OPEN NEAT

National English Ability Test

SPEAKING
Level ①

유형 미리 보기

Part마다 문제 유형별로 예시 문제부터
문제 해결하기까지 제시합니다.

문제 보기 – 문제 풀이 – 문제 파고들기 –
문제 해결하기의 흐름을 따라 가다 보면
문제 유형 파악 끝!

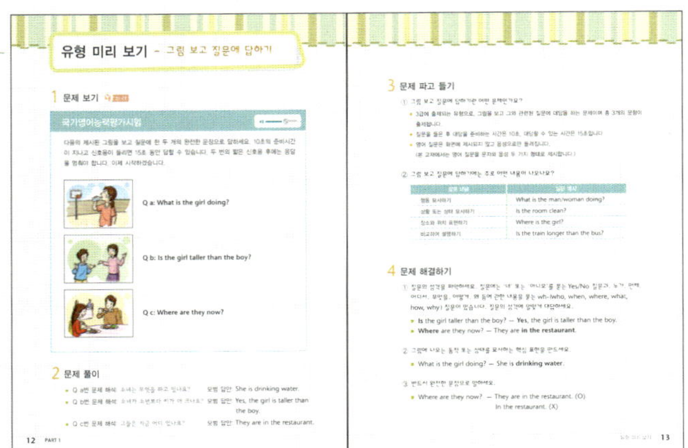

중요 표현 익히기 – 표현 연습

Unit별 말하기에 필요한 중요 표현을
익히고 이를 표현 연습에서
문제로 풀어봅니다.

문제 유형별로 필요한 필수 표현들
습득 완료!

기본 말하기

중요 표현 패턴 연습으로 말하기의
첫걸음 시작!

심화 말하기

문장 단위 말하기로 자신감 상승!

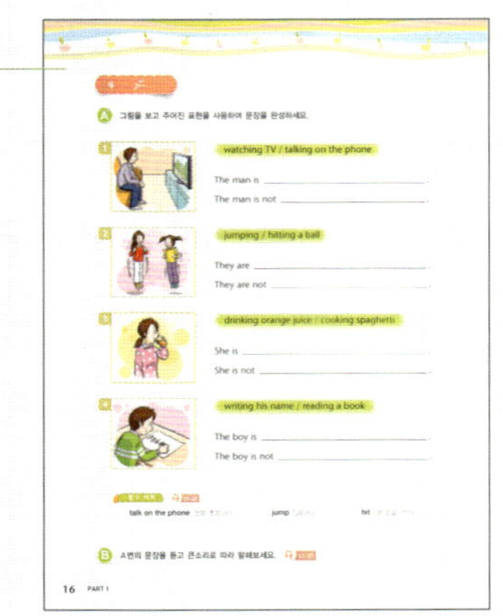

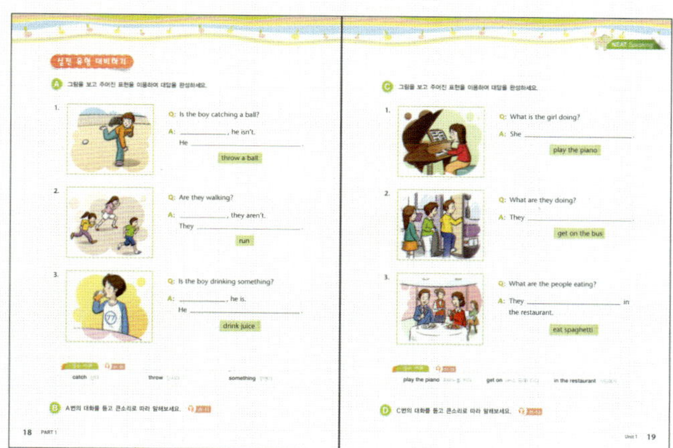

• 실전 유형 대비하기

여러 표현을 익혔으니 이제는 2개의
문제를 통해 실전 유형을 대비합니다.
실제 NEAT 시험 환경처럼 문제를
오디오로도 제공합니다.

많이 풀어 볼수록 내 실력은 쑥쑥!

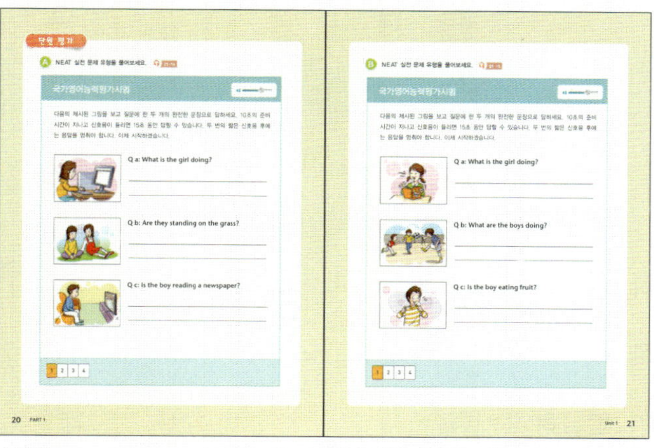

• 단원 평가

한 Unit이 끝날 때 마다 2개의 실전 유형
문제를 풀어봅니다.

실전 문제 유형에 익숙해지기 완료!

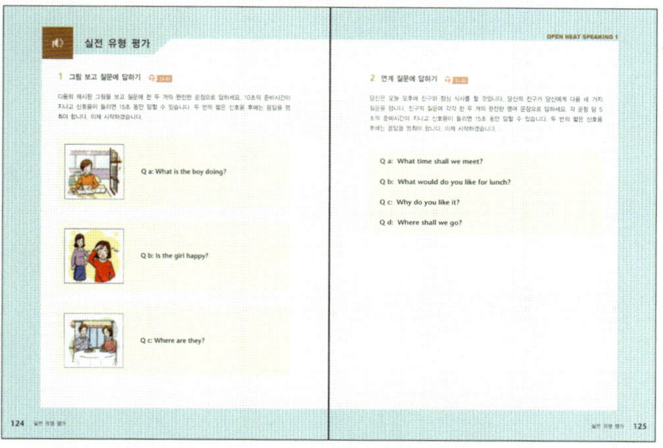

• 실전 유형 평가

4개의 Part에서 배운 유형별 문제를
총망라한 4개의 문제를 풀어보며
나의 실전 유형 풀이 능력을 점검해봅니다.

NEAT SPEAKING 실력 만들기와
실전 감각 훈련 완성!

OPEN NEAT Level 1

SPEAKING 🔊   차례

I. NEAT(National English Ability Test)란 무엇인가요?

1. NEAT의 개요

- NEAT란 국가영어능력평가의 영자 표기로 언어의 4가지 기능인 듣기, 읽기, 말하기, 쓰기를 모두 평가하고 그 중에서도 특히 말하기와 쓰기를 직접 평가함으로써 학생들이 실질적인 영어 의사 소통 능력을 기를 수 있도록 교육하고 이를 평가하는 시험입니다.

2. NEAT의 시험 방식

영역	시험 방식
듣기	헤드셋을 통해 듣고 읽으며 화면의 답안 선택
읽기	화면의 지문을 읽고 답안 선택
말하기	화면의 문제를 듣고 읽으며 헤드셋을 사용하여 직접 음성 답안 녹음
쓰기	화면의 문제를 보고 컴퓨터 키보드를 사용하여 직접 답안 입력

II. NEAT 3급과 2급의 차이가 무엇인가요?

3급	2급
주로 일상 소재를 다루며 공교육 성취 수준과 일상 생활에 필요한 실용 영어 사용 능력을 평가합니다.	기초 학술문을 포함한 일상 소재를 다루며 공교육 성취 수준과 대학에서 학업에 필요한 기본적인 영어 사용 능력을 평가합니다.

★ **3급**

	문제 유형	비율(%)	문항 수	시험 시간
듣기	적절한 응답 찾기	15~20	32	40분
	주제, 제목, 요지, 목적, 의견 찾기	25~30		
	내용 일치 / 불일치, 요청 (요구, 부탁한 일), 이유, 화자가 할 일 찾기 등	35~40		
	그림 고르기, 그림 일치 / 불일치, 위치, 도표 정보 찾기 등	15~20		
읽기	주제, 제목, 요지, 목적, 주장 찾기	30~35	32	50분
	세부 정보 파악 (내용 일치 / 불일치 등)	30~35		
	빈칸 채우기	15~20		
	내용 또는 그림 순서 파악	10~15		
	어구의 함축적 의미 / 지칭 추론	5~10		
말하기	그림 보고 질문에 답하기		1 (3개)	15분
	연계 질문에 답하기		1 (4개)	
	그림 묘사하기		1	
	문제 해결하기		1	
쓰기	상황에 맞는 짧은 글쓰기		1	35분
	그림의 세부 묘사 완성하기		1	
	편지 쓰기		1	
	그림 묘사 및 추론하여 글쓰기		1	

* 시험 시간은 휴식 시간 등을 제외한 시간입니다.

★ 2급

	문제 유형	비율(%)	문항 수	시험 시간
듣기	적절한 응답 찾기	10~15	32	40분
	주제, 제목, 요지, 목적, 의견 찾기	30~35		
	내용 일치 / 불일치, 요청 (요구, 부탁한 일), 이유, 화자가 할 일 찾기 등	35~40		
	위치, 도표 정보 찾기 등	15~20		
읽기	주제, 제목, 요지, 목적, 주장 찾기	30~35	32	50분
	세부 정보 파악 (내용 일치 / 불일치 등)	30~35		
	빈칸 채우기	15~20		
	문장 끼워 넣기	5~10		
	내용 순서 파악	5~10		
	어구의 함축적 의미 / 지칭 추론	5~10		
말하기	연계 질문에 답하기		1 (4개)	15분
	그림 묘사하기		1	
	발표하기		1	
	문제 해결하기		1	
쓰기	일상생활에 관한 글쓰기		1	35분
	자신의 의견 쓰기		1	

* 시험 시간은 휴식 시간 등을 제외한 시간입니다.

III. NEAT 이런 점이 궁금해요.

1. NEAT 공부 따로 준비해야 하나요?

🪁 시험이란 막연히 공부하는 것이 아닙니다.
정확하게 무엇이 나오는지, 어떻게 푸는 건지를 알고 철저히 대비를 해야
능력껏 제 실력을 발휘할 수 있답니다.

2. NEAT 공부 언제부터 시작해야 하나요?

🪁 NEAT는 기존 수능의 듣기, 읽기 시험과는 달리 직접적으로 말하기와 쓰기를
평가하므로 '중학생이 되면 해야지', '고등학생 때 하면 되겠지'라고 생각하면 늦습니다.
영어 학습을 경험하는 순간부터가 NEAT 공부의 시작점입니다.

3. 영어로 말하고 쓰기에 자신이 없는데 어떡해야 하나요?

🪁 많은 연습만이 해결방법인데요, 직접 내 목소리를 녹음해서 들어보고,
간단한 것이더라도 영작해보는 습관을 들여보세요. 어떤 표현을 배웠다면
자꾸 소리 내어 말해 보고 영작하다 보면 자신감과 함께 실력도 쌓인답니다.

4. 컴퓨터로 보는 시험이라는데 어떻게 준비해야 하나요?

🪁 NEAT는 일반 학교에 설치된 컴퓨터실에서 인터넷을 통해
중앙센터서버에 접속하여 치르는 시험입니다.
그렇기에 영어로 타자 치는 것부터 키보드, 마우스, 헤드셋 등을
이용한 실제 컴퓨터 환경에서
훈련을 해두는 것이 필요합니다.

OPEN NEAT

그림 보고 질문에 답하기

차례

유형 미리 보기 – 그림 보고 질문에 답하기

1 문제 보기 

국가영어능력평가시험

다음의 제시된 그림을 보고 질문에 한 두 개의 완전한 문장으로 답하세요. 10초의 준비시간이 지나고 신호음이 들리면 15초 동안 답할 수 있습니다. 두 번의 짧은 신호음 후에는 응답을 멈춰야 합니다. 이제 시작하겠습니다.

Q a: What is the girl doing?

Q b: Is the girl taller than the boy?

Q c: Where are they now?

2 문제 풀이

- Q a번 문제 해석: 소녀는 무엇을 하고 있나요?   모범 답안: She is drinking water.
- Q b번 문제 해석: 소녀가 소년보다 키가 더 크나요? 모범 답안: Yes, the girl is taller than the boy.
- Q c번 문제 해석: 그들은 지금 어디 있나요?   모범 답안: They are in the restaurant.

3 문제 파고 들기

① 그림 보고 질문에 답하기란 어떤 문제인가요?

- 3급에 출제되는 유형으로, 그림을 보고 그와 관련된 질문에 대답을 하는 문제이며 총 3개의 문항이 출제됩니다.
- 질문을 들은 후 대답을 준비하는 시간은 10초, 대답할 수 있는 시간은 15초입니다.
- 영어 질문은 화면에 제시되지 않고 음성으로만 들려집니다.
  (본 교재에서는 영어 질문을 문자와 음성 두 가지 형태로 제시합니다.)

② 그림 보고 질문에 답하기에는 주로 어떤 내용이 나오나요?

질문 내용	질문 예시
행동 묘사하기	What is the man/woman doing?
상황 또는 상태 묘사하기	Is the room clean?
장소와 위치 표현하기	Where is the girl?
비교하여 설명하기	Is the train longer than the bus?

4 문제 해결하기

① 질문의 성격을 파악하세요. 질문에는 '네' 또는 '아니오'를 묻는 Yes/No 질문과, 누가, 언제, 어디서, 무엇을, 어떻게, 왜 등에 관한 내용을 묻는 wh-(who, when, where, what, how, why) 질문이 있습니다. 질문의 성격에 알맞게 대답하세요.

- **Is** the girl taller than the boy? — **Yes**, the girl is taller than the boy.
- **Where** are they now? — They are **in the restaurant**.

② 그림에 나오는 동작 또는 상태를 묘사하는 핵심 표현을 만드세요.

- What is the girl doing? — She is **drinking water**.

③ 반드시 완전한 문장으로 말하세요.

- Where are they now? — They are in the restaurant. (O)
                                                In the restaurant. (X)

그림 속 동작 묘사하기

중요 표현 익히기

A 여러 동작을 나타내는 동사를 익혀봅시다.

● 다음 단어를 듣고 큰소리로 따라 말해보세요.  01-02

run

watch

jump

sit

smile

cook

drink

talk

read

write

laugh

carry

B '지금 ~을 하고 있다'를 표현하는 현재 진행 시제를 익혀봅시다.

● 다음 질문과 대답을 듣고 큰소리로 따라 말해보세요.  01-03

Question	Answer
What **is** she do**ing**?	She **is** run**ning** in the park.
	She **is** cook**ing**.
What **are** they do**ing**?	They **are** watch**ing** TV.
	They **are** talk**ing**.
Is he jump**ing** high?	Yes, he **is** jump**ing** high.
	No, he **is not** jump**ing** high.

표현 연습

A 보기의 단어를 이용하여 현재 진행 시제로 문장을 완성하세요.

① 

②

③ 

④ 

| sit | read | cook | talk |

1. A woman _________________ in the kitchen.

2. They _________________ books at the desk.

3. A boy and a girl _________________ to each other.

4. People _________________ on the grass.

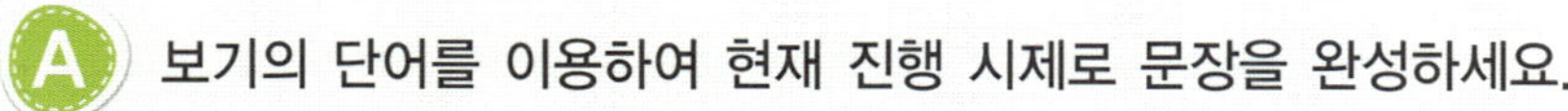

필수 어휘 01-04

each other 서로   **people** 사람들   **grass** 잔디

B A번의 문장을 듣고 큰소리로 따라 말해보세요. 01-05

A 그림을 보고 주어진 표현을 사용하여 문장을 완성하세요.

1 

watching TV / talking on the phone

The man is _________________________.

The man is not _________________________.

2 

jumping / hitting a ball

They are _________________________.

They are not _________________________.

3 

drinking orange juice / cooking spaghetti

She is _________________________.

She is not _________________________.

4 

writing his name / reading a book

The boy is _________________________.

The boy is not _________________________.

필수 어휘  01-06

talk on the phone 전화 통화하다　　　　**jump** 점프하다　　　　**hit** (공 등을) 치다

B A번의 문장을 듣고 큰소리로 따라 말해보세요. 01-07

16　PART 1

심화 말하기

A 그림을 보고 보기의 단어를 이용하여 문장을 완성하세요.

drink	eat	watch	read	carry

1. The old man ____________ coffee.

2. The man ____________ fruit.

3. The boy ____________ TV.

4. The woman ____________ some food.

5. The girl ____________ a magazine.

필수 어휘 01-08

fruit 과일   **carry** ~을 나르다   **magazine** 잡지

B A번의 문장을 듣고 큰소리로 따라 말해보세요. 01-09

A 그림을 보고 주어진 표현을 이용하여 대답을 완성하세요.

1.

Q : Is the boy catching a ball?

A : ______________ , he isn't.

He ________________________________ .

throw a ball

2.

Q : Are they walking?

A : ______________ , they aren't.

They ________________________________ .

run

3.

Q : Is the boy drinking something?

A : ______________ , he is.

He ________________________________ .

drink juice

필수 어휘　01-10

catch 잡다　　　　　throw 던지다　　　　　something 무언가

B A번의 대화를 듣고 큰소리로 따라 말해보세요.　01-11

C 그림을 보고 주어진 표현을 이용하여 대답을 완성하세요.

1.

Q: What is the girl doing?

A: She ________________________________ .

play the piano

2.

Q: What are they doing?

A: They ________________________________ .

get on the bus

3.

Q: What are the people eating?

A: They ________________________ in the restaurant.

eat spaghetti

필수 어휘    01-12

play the piano 피아노를 치다   **get on** (버스 등에) 타다   **in the restaurant** 식당에서

D C번의 대화를 듣고 큰소리로 따라 말해보세요.    01-13

A NEAT 실전 문제 유형을 풀어보세요.  01-14

국가영어능력평가시험 

다음의 제시된 그림을 보고 질문에 한 두 개의 완전한 문장으로 답하세요. 10초의 준비 시간이 지나고 신호음이 들리면 15초 동안 답할 수 있습니다. 두 번의 짧은 신호음 후에는 응답을 멈춰야 합니다. 이제 시작하겠습니다.

Q a: What is the girl doing?

____

____

Q b: Are they standing on the grass?

____

____

Q c: Is the boy reading a newspaper?

____

____

| 1 | 2 | 3 | 4 |

국가영어능력평가시험

다음의 제시된 그림을 보고 질문에 한 두 개의 완전한 문장으로 답하세요. 10초의 준비 시간이 지나고 신호음이 들리면 15초 동안 답할 수 있습니다. 두 번의 짧은 신호음 후에는 응답을 멈춰야 합니다. 이제 시작하겠습니다.

Q a: What is the girl doing?

____

____

Q b: What are the boys doing?

____

____

Q c: Is the boy eating fruit?

____

____

1 2 3 4

그림 속 상태 묘사하기

중요 표현 익히기

A 상태를 나타내는 형용사를 익혀봅시다.

● 다음 단어를 듣고 큰소리로 따라 말해보세요.  02-01

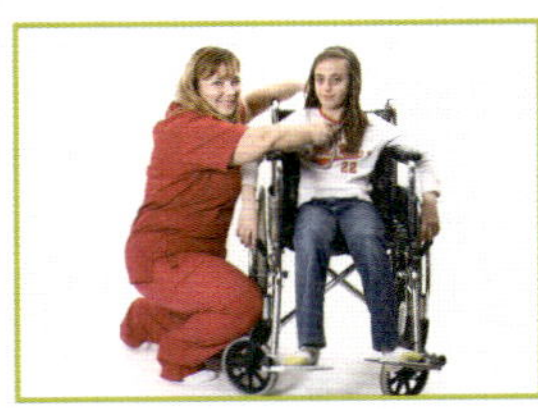

kind

rude

clean

dirty

windy

cloudy

warm

cold

delicious

spicy

interesting

boring

B '~ 이다/다'를 의미하는 'be동사 + 형용사'의 표현을 익혀봅시다.

● 다음 질문과 대답을 듣고 큰소리로 따라 말해보세요.  02-02

Question	Answer
Is he **kind**?	Yes, he is **kind**.
	No, he is **not kind**. He is **rude**.
Is the movie **interesting**?	Yes, it is **interesting**.
	No, it is **not interesting**. It's **boring**.
How is the food?	It is **delicious**. / It is **spicy**.
How's the weather today?	It is **windy**. / It is **cloudy**.

표현 연습

 **A** 보기의 표현을 사용하여 문장을 완성하세요.

① 

② 

③ 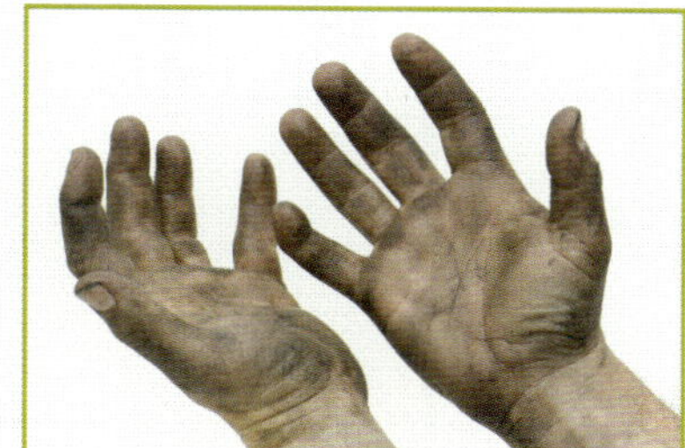

④ 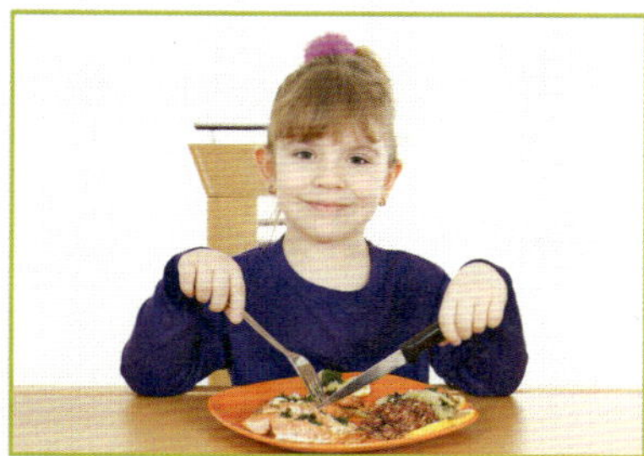

| kind | dirty | delicious | cold |

1. The weather is very ______________ .

2. The girl is so ______________ .

3. The hands are too ______________ .

4. The food is ______________ .

필수 어휘 02-03

kind 친절한	**dirty** 더러운	**delicious** 맛있는
weather 날씨	**so** 매우	**too** 너무

 **B** A번의 문장을 듣고 큰소리로 따라 말해보세요.  02-04

A 그림을 보고 주어진 표현을 사용하여 문장을 완성하세요.

1 

interesting / boring

The game is ______________________.

The game is not ______________________.

2

warm / cold

It is ______________________.

It is not ______________________.

3

kind / rude

The boy is ______________________.

The boy is not ______________________.

4

clean / dirty

The room is ______________________.

The room is not ______________________.

필수 어휘  02-05

interesting 재미있는	**boring** 지루한	**warm** 따뜻한
rude 버릇없는	**clean** 깨끗한	**dirty** 더러운

B A번의 문장을 듣고 큰소리로 따라 말해보세요.  02-06

A 그림을 보고 보기의 단어를 사용하여 문장을 완성하세요.

| kind | rude | sleepy | pretty | windy |

1. It is ______________ today.

2. The boy is ______________ .

3. The girl is ______________ .

4. The boy is ______________ .

5. Her dress is ______________ .

필수 어휘  02-07

kind 친절한   **sleepy** 졸린   **pretty** 예쁜
windy 바람 부는   **dress** 여자 원피스

B A번의 문장을 듣고 큰소리로 따라 말해보세요. 02-08

A 그림을 보고 주어진 표현을 이용하여 대답을 완성하세요.

1.

Q: Is the boy tired?

A: ______________ , he __________________ .

tired

2.

Q: Is the girl sad?

A: ______________ , she isn't.

She __________________ .

happy

3.

Q: Is it warm outside?

A: ______________ , it isn't.

It __________________ outside.

cold

필수 어휘   02-09

tired 지친	warm 따뜻한	outside (건물이 아닌) 밖에

B A번의 대화를 듣고 큰소리로 따라 말해보세요.   02-10

C 그림을 보고 주어진 표현을 사용하여 대답을 완성하세요.

1.

Q: How is the concert?

A: The concert ___________________________.

exciting

2.

Q: How is the weather now?

A: It ___________________________.

sunny and hot

3.

Q: How does he look?

A: He ___________________________.

healthy

필수 어휘  02-11

concert 콘서트	**exciting** 신나는	**sunny** 화창한
hot 더운	**How ~ look?** ~은 어때 보이니?	**healthy** 건강한

D C번의 대화를 듣고 큰소리로 따라 말해보세요.  02-12

 NEAT 실전 문제 유형을 풀어보세요.  02-13

국가영어능력평가시험 

다음의 제시된 그림을 보고 질문에 한 두 개의 완전한 문장으로 답하세요. 10초의 준비 시간이 지나고 신호음이 들리면 15초 동안 답할 수 있습니다. 두 번의 짧은 신호음 후에는 응답을 멈춰야 합니다. 이제 시작하겠습니다.

Q a: What color is the umbrella?

____

____

Q b: Is the food delicious?

____

____

Q c: Is the book interesting?

____

____

국가영어능력평가시험

다음의 제시된 그림을 보고 질문에 한 두 개의 완전한 문장으로 답하세요. 10초의 준비 시간이 지나고 신호음이 들리면 15초 동안 답할 수 있습니다. 두 번의 짧은 신호음 후에는 응답을 멈춰야 합니다. 이제 시작하겠습니다.

Q a: How is the test?

____

____

Q b: How is the weather?

____

____

Q c : Is the girl happy?

____

____

1　2　3　4

그림 속 장소 / 위치 설명하기

중요 표현 익히기

A 장소와 관련된 명사를 익혀봅시다.

● 다음 단어를 듣고 큰소리로 따라 말해보세요.  03-01

building

bookstore

park

bus stop

office

fire station

supermarket

police station

library

playground

restaurant

bridge

B 위치를 나타내는 '전치사 + 사물'의 표현을 익혀봅시다.

● 다음 문장을 듣고 큰소리로 따라 말해보세요. 03-02

전치사	뜻	예문
at	~에	They are **at** the bus stop.
in	~ 안에	She is **in** the office.
on	~ 위에	It is **on** the desk.
under	~ 아래에	No, it is not **under** the table.
next to	~ 옆에	Yes, it is **next to** the park.
in front of	~ 앞에	A bookstore is **in front of** the school.

표현 연습

A 보기의 표현을 사용하여 문장을 완성하세요.

① 
② 
③ 
④ 

| in | on | next to | in front of |

1. The cars are ______________ the building.

2. The girl is studying ______________ the library.

3. They are walking ______________ the bridge.

4. The woman is standing ______________ the bus stop.

필수 어휘  03-03

next to ~ 옆에	**in front of** ~ 앞에	**building** 건물
library 도서관	**bridge** 다리	**bus stop** 버스 정류장

B A번의 문장을 듣고 큰소리로 따라 말해보세요.  03-04

A 그림을 보고 주어진 표현을 사용하여 문장을 완성하세요.

1

on / under

The laptop computer is _____________ the table.

The laptop computer is not _____________ the table.

2

in / next to

They are playing _____________ the water.

They are not playing _____________ the water.

3

in front of / in

The man is _____________ the building.

The man is not _____________ the building.

4

under / on

They are sitting _____________ the parasol.

They are not sitting _____________ the parasol.

필수 어휘  03-05

under ~ 아래에	**laptop computer** 노트북 컴퓨터	**next to** ~ 옆에
in the water 물속에서	**building** 건물	**parasol** 파라솔

B A번의 문장을 듣고 큰소리로 따라 말해보세요. 03-06

A 그림을 보고 주어진 표현을 사용하여 문장을 완성하세요.

in	at	on	next to

1. A boy is buying flowers _____________ the flower shop.

2. A man is sitting _____________ the chair.

3. A woman is eating _____________ the restaurant.

4. A man is standing _____________ the car.

필수 어휘   03-07

| buy 사다 | flower shop 꽃 가게 | sit 앉다 |
| eat 먹다 | stand 서 있다 | |

B A번의 문장을 듣고 큰소리로 따라 말해보세요.   03-08

A 그림을 보고 주어진 표현을 이용하여 대답을 완성하세요.

1.

Q: Is the man working in the office?

A: Yes, he is working

__________________________ .

in

2.

Q: Are the children reading books in the bookstore?

A: No, they aren't. They are playing

__________________________ .

on

3.

Q: Is the girl eating in the restaurant?

A: No, she isn't. She is waiting for the bus

__________________________ .

at

필수 어휘  03-09

office 사무실	**bookstore** 서점	**playground** 놀이터
wait for ~을 기다리다	**bus stop** 버스 정류장	

B A번의 대화를 듣고 큰소리로 따라 말해보세요.  03-10

C 그림을 보고 주어진 표현을 이용하여 대답을 완성하세요.

1.

Q: Where are the trees?

A: They are _______________________ .

next to

2.

Q: Where are they now?

A: They are _______________________ .

at

3.

Q: Where is the man standing?

A: He is standing _______________________ .

in front of

필수 어휘    03-11

bookstore 서점	**supermarket** 슈퍼마켓	**police station** 경찰서

D C번의 대화를 듣고 큰소리로 따라 말해보세요.   03-12

A NEAT 실전 문제 유형을 풀어보세요.  03-13

국가영어능력평가시험 

다음의 제시된 그림을 보고 질문에 한 두 개의 완전한 문장으로 답하세요. 10초의 준비 시간이 지나고 신호음이 들리면 15초 동안 답할 수 있습니다. 두 번의 짧은 신호음 후에는 응답을 멈춰야 합니다. 이제 시작하겠습니다.

Q a: Where are they now?

____

____

Q b: Are they playing in the park?

____

____

Q c: Where is the bus stop?

____

____

1 2 3 4

국가영어능력평가시험

다음의 제시된 그림을 보고 질문에 한 두 개의 완전한 문장으로 답하세요. 10초의 준비 시간이 지나고 신호음이 들리면 15초 동안 답할 수 있습니다. 두 번의 짧은 신호음 후에 는 응답을 멈춰야 합니다. 이제 시작하겠습니다.

Q a: Where is the girl studying?

____

____

Q b: Where is the cat?

____

____

Q c: Are they in the classroom?

____

____

| 1 | 2 | 3 | 4 |

OPEN NEAT

연계 질문에 답하기

차례

- 유형 미리 보기
- **Unit 4** 학교 생활
- **Unit 5** 가정 생활
- **Unit 6** 사회 활동
- **Unit 7** 여가 생활

유형 미리 보기 – 연계 질문에 답하기

1 문제 보기  04-01

당신은 오늘 오후 친구와 함께 영화를 볼 계획입니다. 당신의 친구는 당신에게 다음 네 가지 질문을 합니다. 친구의 질문에 각각 한 두 개의 완전한 영어 문장으로 답하세요. 각 문항당 10초의 준비시간이 지나고 신호음이 들리면 15초 동안 답할 수 있습니다. 두 번의 짧은 신호음 후에는 응답을 멈추어야 합니다. 이제 시작하겠습니다.

Q a: What movie would you like to see?

Q b: Where shall we meet?

Q c: When shall we meet?

Q d: How can we get to the theater?

2 문제 풀이

- 질문 해석 a: 당신은 어떤 영화를 보고 싶나요?
  모범 답안 a: **I'd like to see an action movie.** 저는 액션 영화를 보고 싶어요.
- 질문 해석 b: 어디에서 만날까요?
  모범 답안 b: **Let's meet in front of the theater.** 극장 앞에서 만나요.
- 질문 해석 c: 언제 만날까요?
  모범 답안 c: **Let's meet at 3 p.m.** 오후 3시에 만나요.
- 질문 해석 d: 극장에는 어떻게 가죠?
  모범 답안 d: **We can get there by bus.** 버스를 타고 가면 돼요.

3 문제 파고 들기

① 연계 질문에 답하기란 어떤 문제인가요?

- 특정 상황이나 주제에 대해 주어지는 4개의 질문에 응답하는 문제입니다. 보통 일상적이고 실용적인 주제가 나옵니다.
- 모니터 화면에 지시문이 나오고, 4개의 하위 문항은 짤막한 질문으로 음성으로만 주어집니다.
- 각 하위 문항에 대한 답을 준비할 수 있는 시간은 3급은 10초, 2급은 5초입니다.
- 삐 소리가 한 번 나면 응답을 시작하세요. 각 문항 당 답변할 시간은 3급에는 15초, 2급에는 20초가 주어지며, 두 번의 삐 소리가 나면 응답을 멈춥니다.

② 연계 질문에 답하기에는 어떤 지시문들이 나오나요?

질문 예시
What do you usually do on Sunday?
When do you play soccer?
What time do you get up?
Where do you want to go?
How can you get there?
Why do you want to do it?
Can you play the piano?

4 문제 해결하기

① 마치 컴퓨터를 앞에 두고 개인 면접을 보듯이 자신의 생각, 경험, 느낌, 의견 등을 표현하도록 합니다.

② 질문을 정확히 파악하여 질문에서 물어보는 내용에 대해 완전한 문장으로 대답하는 데 초점을 두세요.

③ 질문에서 묻지 않는 내용을 답한다고 해서 추가 점수를 받는 것은 아닙니다.

④ 평소에 가족이나 친구들과 일상적이고 실용적인 주제에 관해 영어로 얘기해 보세요. 자신의 생각과 의견을 말하는 연습을 많이 하면 이러한 시험 유형에 자신감을 가질 수 있습니다.

학교 생활

A 학교 생활과 관련된 여러 표현을 익혀봅시다.

● 다음 표현을 듣고 큰소리로 따라 말해보세요.  04-02

go to school

class

classmate

homeroom teacher

teach

take a lesson

take an exam

study

have lunch

B '~하다'를 표현하는 현재 시제를 익혀봅시다.

● 다음 질문과 대답을 듣고 큰소리로 따라 말해보세요. 04-03

Question	Answer
What time **do** you **go** to school?	I **go** to school at 8 a.m.
How many classes **do** you **have** a day?	I **have** five classes a day.
How **do** you **get** to school?	I **get** to school on foot.
Where **do** you **study**?	I **study** in the library.
What **do** you **have** for lunch?	I **have** a sandwich for lunch.
When **do** you **play** soccer?	I **play** soccer after class.

표현 연습

A 그림 속 인물이 '나'라고 생각하고 현재 시제로 문장을 완성하세요.

① 

②

③ 

④

| have lunch | take an exam | study | take a violin lesson |

1. I ___________________________ in the library.

2. I ___________________________ .

3. I ___________________________ .

4. I ___________________________ with my friends.

필수 어휘　🎧 04-04

have lunch 점심을 먹다　　**take an exam** 시험을 치다　　**take a lesson** 수업을 받다

B A번의 문장을 듣고 큰소리로 따라 말해보세요.　🎧 04-05

A 당신은 친구와 학교 생활에 대해 대화를 나누고 있습니다. 당신의 친구는 당신에게 다음 네 가지 질문을 합니다. 주어진 표현을 모두 사용하여 각각 두 개의 완전한 영어 문장으로 답하세요.

1
- at 8:30
- at about 8 o'clock

Q: What time do you go to school?

A: I go to school ___________________________ .

/ I go to school ___________________________ .

2
- five classes
- seven classes

Q: How many classes do you have a day?

A: I have ___________________ a day.

/ I have ___________________ a day.

3
- very nice
- friendly

Q: How are your classmates?

A: They're ___________________ .

/ They're ___________________ .

4
- study in the library
- take a piano lesson

Q: What do you do after class?

A: I ___________________ .

/ I ___________________ .

필수 어휘  04-06

| **about** 대략 | **class** 수업 | **a day** 하루에 |
| **friendly** 다정한 | **after class** 방과 후에 | **take a piano lesson** 피아노 수업을 받다 |

B A번의 대화를 듣고 큰소리로 따라 말해보세요. 04-07

심화 말하기

A 당신은 친구와 다음 수업 시간에 대해 대화를 나누고 있습니다. 당신의 친구는 당신에게 다음 네 가지 질문을 합니다. 주어진 표현을 모두 사용하여 각각 두 개의 완전한 영어 문장으로 답하세요.

1
- English
- math

Q: What is your next class?

A: It's ___________________________ .

/ It's ___________________________ .

2
- Mr. Johnson
- Ms. Jung

Q: Who teaches the class?

A: ___________________________ teaches the class.

/ ___________________________ teaches the class.

3
- great
- kind

Q: How is he/she?

A: He/She is ___________________________ .

/ He/She is ___________________________ .

4
- at 3 p.m.
- at 5 in the afternoon

Q: When do you finish the class?

A: I finish the class ___________________________ .

/ I finish the class ___________________________ .

필수 어휘   04-08

next 다음	**class** 수업	**teach** 가르치다
great 훌륭한	**in the afternoon** 오후에	

B A번의 대화를 듣고 큰소리로 따라 말해보세요. 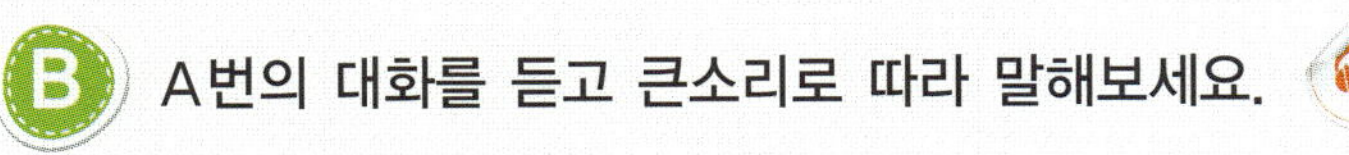 04-09

A 당신은 친구와 학교 생활에 대해 대화를 나누고 있습니다. 당신의 친구는 당신에게 다음 네 가지 질문을 합니다. 주어진 표현을 사용하여 완전한 영어 문장으로 답하세요.

1. **Q a** When is lunch time?

   Your answer   It is _______________________ .

   from 12:30 to 1:30

2. **Q b** Where do you have lunch?

   Your answer   I have lunch _______________________ .

   in the school cafeteria

3. **Q c** What classes do you have in the afternoon?

   Your answer   I have _______________________ .

   PE and art class

4. **Q d** What will you do after class?

   Your answer   I will _______________________ with my friends.

   play soccer

필수 어휘  04-10

lunch time 점심 시간	**school cafeteria** 학교 식당	**PE** 체육 시간
art 미술	**play soccer** 축구를 하다	

B A번의 대화를 듣고 큰소리로 따라 말해보세요.  04-11

C 당신은 친구와 좋아하는 과목에 대해 대화를 나누고 있습니다. 당신의 친구는 당신에게 다음 네 가지 질문을 합니다. 주어진 표현을 사용하여 완전한 영어 문장으로 답하세요.

1. **Q a**   What is your favorite subject?

   Your answer   My favorite subject ________________________ .

   English

2. **Q b**   Why do you like it?

   Your answer   It ____________________ .

   interesting

3. **Q c**   Who teaches it?

   Your answer   ____________________ it.

   Kate

4. **Q d**   How is the teacher?

   Your answer   She ____________________ .

   helpful

 필수 어휘   04-12

favorite 가장 좋아하는   **subject** 과목   **helpful** 도움이 되는

D C번의 대화를 듣고 큰소리로 따라 말해보세요.   04-13

 NEAT 실전 문제 유형을 풀어보세요.  04-14

국가영어능력평가시험 

당신과 친구는 아침에 등교하는 것에 대해 대화를 나누고 있습니다. 당신의 친구는 당신에게 다음 네 가지 질문을 합니다. 친구의 질문에 각각 한 두 개의 완전한 영어 문장으로 답하세요. 각 문항 당 10초의 준비시간이 지나고 신호음이 들리면 15초 동안 답할 수 있습니다. 두 번의 짧은 신호음 후에는 응답을 멈추어야 합니다. 이제 시작하겠습니다.

Q a: When do you go to school?

Q b: How do you get to school?

Q c: How long does it take?

Q d: What time does your first class start?

1 2 3 4

국가영어능력평가시험

당신은 친구와 학교생활에 대해 대화를 나누고 있습니다. 당신의 친구는 당신에게 다음 네 가지 질문을 합니다. 친구의 질문에 각각 한 두 개의 완전한 영어 문장으로 답하세요. 각 문항 당 10초의 준비시간이 지나고 신호음이 들리면 15초 동안 답할 수 있습니다. 두 번의 짧은 신호음 후에는 응답을 멈추어야 합니다. 이제 시작하겠습니다.

Q a: When does your class begin?

Q b: How many classes do you have a day?

Q c: What is your favorite subject?

Q d: Why do you like the subject?

1 2 3 4

가정 생활

A 가정 생활과 관련된 표현들을 익혀봅시다.

● 다음 표현을 듣고 큰소리로 따라 말해보세요.  05-01

get up

go to sleep

take a shower

have breakfast

help my mom

wash the dishes

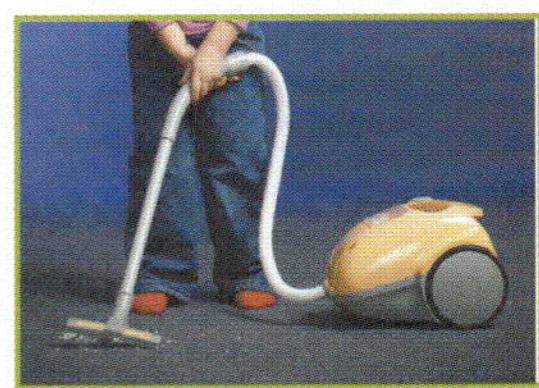
clean the room

take a walk

do my homework

B 가정 생활과 관련된 질문과 대답을 익혀봅시다.

● 다음 질문과 대답을 듣고 큰소리로 따라 말해보세요.  05-02

Question	Answer
What time do you get up?	I usually get up **at 7:30**.
Do you have breakfast?	**Yes**, I always have breakfast.
Who do you help?	I help **my mom**.
Where do you do your homework?	I do my homework **in my room**.
When do you clean your room?	I clean my room **in the morning**.
How often do you take a walk?	I take a walk **three times a week**.

표현 연습

A 그림 속 인물이 '나'라고 생각하고 현재 시제로 문장을 완성하세요.

① 

②

③ 

④ 

| clean the room | wash the dishes | take a walk | take a shower |

1. I _________________________________ .

2. I _________________________________ .

3. I _________________________________ .

4. I _________________________ with my dog.

필수 어휘 05-03

clean the room 방을 청소하다   **wash the dishes** 설거지를 하다
take a walk 산책하다   **take a shower** 샤워하다

B A번의 문장을 듣고 큰소리로 따라 말해보세요. 05-04

A 당신은 친구와 가정 생활에 대해 대화를 나누고 있습니다. 당신의 친구는 당신에게 다음 네 가지 질문을 합니다. 주어진 표현을 모두 사용하여 각각 두 개의 완전한 영어 문장으로 답하세요.

1
- at 7 o'clock
- at 7:40

Q: What time do you get up?

A: I get up ___________________ .

/ I get up ___________________ .

2
- cereal
- toast and juice

Q: What do you have for breakfast?

A: I have ___________________ for breakfast.

/ I have ___________________ for breakfast.

3
- clean my room
- wash the dishes

Q: What do you do after dinner?

A: I ___________________ .

/ I ___________________ .

4
- at 10 o'clock
- after 10

Q: When do you go to sleep?

A: I go to sleep ___________________ .

/ I go to sleep ___________________ .

필수 어휘 05-05

get up 일어나다	**for breakfast** 아침식사로	**cereal** 시리얼
toast 토스트	**wash the dishes** 설거지하다	**after dinner** 저녁식사 후에

B A번의 대화를 듣고 큰소리로 따라 말해보세요. 05-06

심화 말하기

A 당신은 친구와 아침에 하는 일에 대해 대화를 나누고 있습니다. 당신의 친구는 당신에게 다음 네 가지 질문을 합니다. 주어진 표현을 모두 사용하여 각각 두 개의 완전한 영어 문장으로 답하세요.

1
- before 7
- at about 7:30

Q: What time do you get up?

A: I get up _________________________.

/ I get up _________________________.

2
- brush my teeth
- wash my face

Q: What do you do first in the morning?

A: I _________________________.

/ I _________________________.

3
- with my family
- with my sister

Q: Who do you have breakfast with?

A: I have breakfast _________________________.

/ I have breakfast _________________________.

4
- after breakfast
- at 8

Q: When do you leave the house for school?

A: I leave the house _________________________.

/ I leave the house _________________________.

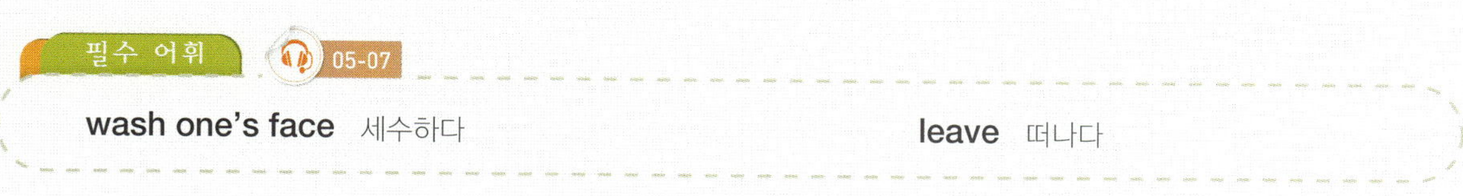

필수 어휘   05-07

wash one's face 세수하다   **leave** 떠나다

B A번의 대화를 듣고 큰소리로 따라 말해보세요.   05-08

A 당신은 친구와 방과 후의 일들에 대해 대화를 나누고 있습니다. 당신의 친구는 당신에게 다음 네 가지 질문을 합니다. 주어진 표현을 사용하여 완전한 영어 문장으로 답하세요.

1. **Q a** When do you come back home from school?

    Your answer   I come back home ___________________________ .

    at about 3 o'clock

2. **Q b** What do you do when you come back home?

    Your answer   I ___________________________ when I come back home.

    take a shower

3. **Q c** Do you also clean your room?

    Your answer   Yes, I ___________________________ .

    clean my room

4. **Q d** What do you do after dinner?

    Your answer   I ___________________________ after dinner.

    take a walk

필수 어휘  05-09

come back home 집에 돌아오다	**take a shower** 샤워를 하다
clean my room 내 방을 청소하다	**take a walk** 산책하다

B A번의 대화를 듣고 큰소리로 따라 말해보세요. 05-10

C 당신은 친구와 집에서 하는 일들에 대해 대화를 나누고 있습니다. 당신의 친구는 당신에게 다음 네 가지 질문을 합니다. 주어진 표현을 사용하여 완전한 영어 문장으로 하세요.

1. **Q a** What do you like to do at home?

   Your answer _______________________________ .

   to watch TV

2. **Q b** What do you do before dinner?

   Your answer _______________________________ .

   do my homework

3. **Q c** Do you help your mom?

   Your answer Yes, _______________________________ after dinner.

   wash the dishes

4. **Q d** When do you go to bed?

   Your answer _______________________________ .

   around 10 o'clock

필수 어휘  05-11

watch TV TV를 보다	**before dinner** 저녁식사 전에	**wash the dishes** 설거지를 하다
go to bed 잠자리에 들다	**around** 대략	

D C번의 대화를 듣고 큰소리로 따라 말해보세요. 05-12

단원 평가

 NEAT 실전 문제 유형을 풀어보세요. 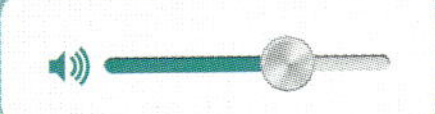

국가영어능력평가시험

당신은 친구와 가정 생활에 대해 대화를 나누고 있습니다. 당신의 친구는 당신에게 다음 네 가지 질문을 합니다. 친구의 질문에 각각 한 두 개의 완전한 영어 문장으로 답하세요. 각 문항 당 10초의 준비시간이 지나고 신호음이 들리면 15초 동안 답할 수 있습니다. 두 번의 짧은 신호음 후에는 응답을 멈추어야 합니다. 이제 시작하겠습니다.

Q a: What time do you wake up?

Q b: Do you have breakfast?

Q c: What do you do before you go to school?

Q d: When do you leave your home?

| 1 | 2 | 3 | 4 |

국가영어능력평가시험

당신은 친구와 방과 후 일과에 대해 대화를 나누고 있습니다. 당신의 친구는 당신에게 다음 네 가지 질문을 합니다. 친구의 질문에 각각 한 두 개의 완전한 영어 문장으로 답하세요. 각 문항 당 10초의 준비시간이 지나고 신호음이 들리면 15초 동안 답할 수 있습니다. 두 번의 짧은 신호음 후에는 응답을 멈추어야 합니다. 이제 시작하겠습니다.

Q a: What time do you come back home?

Q b: What do you do after you come back home?

Q c: What do you do after dinner?

Q d: When do you go to sleep?

1 2 3 4

사회 활동

A 사회 생활과 관련한 표현들을 익혀봅시다.

● 다음 표현을 듣고 큰소리로 따라 말해보세요. 06-01

introduce

visit

work

meet

have a chat

join a club

invite

wait for

have a meal

B 사회 활동과 관련된 질문과 대답을 익혀봅시다.

● 다음 질문과 대답을 듣고 큰소리로 따라 말해보세요. 06-02

Question	Answer
What do you usually do with your friends?	I **have a chat** with my friends.
Where do you wait for Sujin?	I wait for Sujin **at the bus stop**.
Who will you meet tomorrow?	I'll meet **my friend, Jessica**.
When do you visit your grandparents?	I visit my grandparents **on weekends**.
Who do you want to invite to the party?	I want to invite **all of my classmates**.

표 현 연 습

A 그림 속 인물이 '나'라고 생각하고 현재 시제로 문장을 완성하세요.

① 

② 

③ 

④ 

| visit | meet | join | introduce |

1. I _________________ myself.

2. I _________________ my grandparents.

3. I'd like to _________________ a drama club.

4. We _________________ our friends at the library.

필수 어휘　06-03

visit ~를 찾아가다　　　　　　**join** ~에 가입하다　　　　　　**introduce** 소개하다
grandparents 할아버지, 할머니　　**drama club** 연극 모임　　　**library** 도서관

B A번의 문장을 듣고 큰소리로 따라 말해보세요.　　06-04

A 당신은 친구와 사회 활동에 대해 대화를 나누고 있습니다. 당신의 친구는 당신에게 다음 네 가지 질문을 합니다. 주어진 표현을 모두 사용하여 각각 두 개의 완전한 영어 문장으로 답하세요.

1
- my friends
- my classmates

Q: Who do you meet outside?

A: I meet _________________________.

/ I meet _________________________.

2
- a library
- a park

Q: Where do you go with them?

A: I go to _________________ with them.

/ I go to _________________ with them.

3
- read books
- take a walk

Q: What do you do with them?

A: I _________________ with them.

/ I _________________ with them.

4
- school life
- our favorite singers

Q: What do you talk about with them?

A: We talk about _________________.

/ We talk about _________________.

필수 어휘 06-05

classmate 같은 반 친구   **take a walk** 산책하다   **school life** 학교 생활
favorite 가장 좋아하는   **singers** 가수들

B A번의 대화를 듣고 큰소리로 따라 말해보세요. 06-06

심화 말하기

A 당신은 친구와 사회 활동에 대해 대화를 나누고 있습니다. 당신의 친구는 당신에게 다음 네 가지 질문을 합니다. 주어진 표현을 모두 사용하여 각각 두 개의 완전한 영어 문장으로 답하세요.

1
- a soccer club
- a dancing club

Q: What club are you in?

A: I am in ________________________ .

/ I am in ________________________ .

2
- play soccer
- practice dancing

Q: What do you do in the club?

A: I ________________________ with my friends.

/ I ________________________ with the club members.

3
- on the playground
- in the gym

Q: Where does your club meet?

A: We meet ________________________ .

/ We meet ________________________ .

4
- good for my health
- make friends

Q: Why are you in the club?

A: Because it is ________________________ .

/ Because I can ________________________ .

필수 어휘  06-07

club 클럽, 동호회	**practice** 연습하다	**club member** 클럽 회원	**playground** 운동장
gym 체육관	**be good for** ~에 좋다	**health** 건강	**make friends** 친구를 사귀다

B A번의 대화를 듣고 큰소리로 따라 말해보세요.  06-08

A 당신은 친구와 생일 파티에 대해 대화를 나누고 있습니다. 당신의 친구는 당신에게 다음 네 가지 질문을 합니다. 주어진 표현을 이용하여 완전한 영어 문장으로 답하세요.

1.　**Q a**　When will you have your birthday party?

　　Your answer　I will have my birthday party ________________ .

this Friday

2.　**Q b**　How many friends will you invite to your party?

　　Your answer　I will invite ________________ .

ten friends

3.　**Q c**　Where will you have your birthday party?

　　Your answer　I will have my birthday party ________________ .

at home

4.　**Q d**　What gift do you want to get?

　　Your answer　I want to get ________________ .

pretty clothes

필수 어휘　06-09

birthday party 생일 파티	**invite** 초대하다	**gift** 선물
get 받다	**pretty** 예쁜	**clothes** 옷

B A번의 대화를 듣고 큰소리로 따라 말해보세요.　06-10

C 당신은 친구와 봉사 활동에 대해 대화를 나누고 있습니다. 당신의 친구는 당신에게 다음 네 가지 질문을 합니다. 주어진 표현을 이용하여 완전한 영어 문장으로 답하세요.

1. **Q a** Do you do any volunteer work?

   Your answer   Yes, ____________________________________.

   help old people

2. **Q b** How often do you do it?

   Your answer   ____________________________________.

   once a week

3. **Q c** Who do you do it with?

   Your answer   ____________________________________.

   my classmates

4. **Q d** How do you feel after the volunteer work?

   Your answer   ____________________________________.

   great

필수 어휘  06-11

volunteer work 봉사활동	**old people** 노인들	**once a week** 일주일에 한번
classmates 반 친구들	**feel** (어떤 감정을) 느끼다	**great** 좋은

D C번의 대화를 듣고 큰소리로 따라 말해보세요.  06-12

 NEAT 실전 문제 유형을 풀어보세요.  06-13

국가영어능력평가시험 

당신은 친구와 저녁식사를 할 식당에 대한 대화를 나누고 있습니다. 당신의 친구는 당신에게 다음 네 가지 질문을 합니다. 친구의 질문에 각각 한 두 개의 완전한 영어 문장으로 답하세요. 각 문항 당 10초의 준비시간이 지나고 신호음이 들리면 15초 동안 답할 수 있습니다. 두 번의 짧은 신호음 후에는 응답을 멈추어야 합니다. 이제 시작하겠습니다.

Q a: What kind of food would you like to eat?

Q b: What kind of restaurant would you like to go to?

Q c: Where is the restaurant?

Q d: How far is the restaurant from here?

1 2 3 4

국가영어능력평가시험 

당신은 친구와 사회 활동에 대해 대화를 나누고 있습니다. 당신의 친구는 당신에게 다음 네 가지 질문을 합니다. 친구의 질문에 각각 한 두 개의 완전한 영어 문장으로 답하세요. 각 문항 당 10초의 준비시간이 지나고 신호음이 들리면 15초 동안 답할 수 있습니다. 두 번의 짧은 신호음 후에는 응답을 멈추어야 합니다. 이제 시작하겠습니다.

Q a: Do you meet your friends outside?

Q b: How often do you meet them?

Q c: Where do you go with them?

Q d: What do you usually do with them?

여가 생활

중요 표현 익히기

A 여가 생활과 관련된 표현을 익혀봅시다.

● 다음 표현을 듣고 큰소리로 따라 말해보세요.  07-01

play the piano

play a game

be interested in

listen to music

like sports

draw a picture

ride a bicycle

see a movie

take a trip

B 사회 활동과 관련된 질문과 대답을 익혀봅시다.

● 다음 질문과 대답을 듣고 큰소리로 따라 말해보세요. 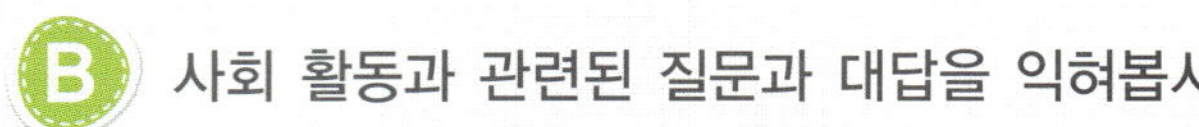 07-02

Question	Answer
What kind of sports do you like?	I like **basketball**.
Who is your favorite singer?	I love **Chad**.
What are you interested in?	I'm interested in **history**.
Why do you play the piano?	I want to be a **pianist**.
Where do you ride a bicycle?	I ride a bicycle **in the park**.
When do you listen to music?	I listen to music **after school**.

표현 연습

A 그림 속 인물이 '나' 라고 생각하고 현재 시제로 문장을 완성하세요.

① 

② 

③

④ 

| am interested in | ride a bicycle | take a trip | draw a picture |

1. I ＿＿＿＿＿＿＿＿＿＿ baseball.

2. I ＿＿＿＿＿＿＿＿＿＿ in my free time.

3. I will ＿＿＿＿＿＿＿＿＿＿ to the beach this weekend.

4. I ＿＿＿＿＿＿＿＿＿＿ for exercise.

필수 어휘  07-03

be interested in ～에 관심이 있다　**ride a bicycle** 자전거를 타다　**take a trip** 여행을 가다
draw a picture 그림을 그리다　**free time** 여가시간　**for exercise** 운동으로

B A번의 문장을 듣고 큰소리로 따라 말해보세요.　07-04

A 당신은 친구와 관심, 흥미에 대해 대화를 나누고 있습니다. 당신의 친구는 당신에게 다음 네 가지 질문을 합니다. 주어진 표현을 모두 사용하여 각각 두 개의 완전한 영어 문장으로 답하세요.

1
- Japan
- France

Q: What country would you like to go to?

A: I'd like to go to ________________________.

I'd like to go to ________________________.

2
- shopping
- French food

Q: Why do you want to go there?

A: I like ________________________.

I like ________________________.

3
- Asia
- Europe

Q: Where is the country?

A: It is in ________________________.

It is in ________________________.

4
- by plane
- by ship

Q: How can you travel to the country?

A: I can travel ________________________.

I can travel ________________________.

필수 어휘  07-05

| country 국가 | France 프랑스 | French 프랑스의 | Asia 아시아 |
| Europe 유럽 | travel to ~로 여행하다 | by plane 비행기로 | by ship 배로 |

B A번의 대화를 듣고 큰소리로 따라 말해보세요.  07-06

심화 말하기

A 당신은 친구와 관심, 흥미에 대해 대화를 나누고 있습니다. 당신의 친구는 당신에게 다음 네 가지 질문을 합니다. 주어진 표현을 모두 사용하여 각각 두 개의 완전한 영어 문장으로 답하세요.

1
- summer
- winter

Q: What is your favorite season?

A: My favorite season is ______________________.

My favorite season is ______________________.

2
- rain
- snow

Q: Why do you like the season?

A: I like ______________________.

I like ______________________.

3
- hot
- cold

Q: What kind of weather do you like?

A: I like ______________________ weather.

I like ______________________ weather.

4
- swimming
- making a snowman

Q: What do you do during the season?

A: I enjoy ______________________.

I enjoy ______________________.

필수 어휘 07-07

season 계절
enjoy -ing ~하는 것을 즐기다

during ~하는 동안
make a snowman 눈사람을 만들다

B A번의 대화를 듣고 큰소리로 따라 말해보세요. 07-08

A 당신은 친구와 관심, 흥미에 대해 대화를 나누고 있습니다. 당신의 친구는 당신에게 다음 네 가지 질문을 합니다. 주어진 표현을 사용하여 완전한 영어 문장으로 답하세요.

1. **Q a** What place would you like to visit?

    Your answer I would like to visit ______________________ .

    the zoo

2. **Q b** What can you see there?

    Your answer I can see ______________________ .

    many kinds of animals

3. **Q c** What is the most popular animal there?

    Your answer ______________________ are the most popular.

    Dolphins

4. **Q d** How can you go there?

    Your answer I can go there ______________________ .

    by subway

필수 어휘  07-09

| visit 방문하다 | zoo 동물원 | many kinds of 많은 종류의 ~ |
| popular 인기 있는 | by subway 지하철을 타고 | |

B A번의 대화를 듣고 큰소리로 따라 말해보세요. 07-10

C 당신은 친구와 관심, 흥미에 대해 대화를 나누고 있습니다. 당신의 친구는 당신에게 다음 네 가지 질문을 합니다. 주어진 표현을 사용하여 완전한 영어 문장으로 답하세요.

1. **Q a** What kinds of sports are popular in Korea?

   Your answer _______________________________.

   Baseball and soccer

2. **Q b** Which sport do you like the most?

   Your answer _______________________________.

   basketball

3. **Q c** Who do you play it with?

   Your answer _______________________________.

   my friends

4. **Q d** How often do you play it?

   Your answer _______________________________.

   every Sunday

필수 어휘  07-11

what kinds of ~ 무슨 종류의	**the most** 가장	**sport** 운동
how often 얼마나 자주	**every Sunday** 일요일마다	

D C번의 대화를 듣고 큰소리로 따라 말해보세요. 07-12

 NEAT 실전 문제 유형을 풀어보세요.  07-13

국가영어능력평가시험 

당신은 친구와 관심, 흥미에 대해 대화를 나누고 있습니다. 당신의 친구는 당신에게 다음 네 가지 질문을 합니다. 친구의 질문에 각각 한 두 개의 완전한 영어 문장으로 답하세요. 각 문항 당 10초의 준비시간이 지나고 신호음이 들리면 15초 동안 답할 수 있습니다. 두 번의 짧은 신호음 후에는 응답을 멈추어야 합니다. 이제 시작하겠습니다.

Q a: What kinds of books do you like the most?

Q b: When do you read?

Q c: Where do you usually read?

Q d: How many books do you read a month?

1 2 3 4

국가영어능력평가시험

당신은 친구와 관심, 흥미에 대해 대화를 나누고 있습니다. 당신의 친구는 당신에게 다음 네 가지 질문을 합니다. 친구의 질문에 각각 한 두 개의 완전한 영어 문장으로 답하세요. 각 문항 당 10초의 준비시간이 지나고 신호음이 들리면 15초 동안 답할 수 있습니다. 두 번의 짧은 신호음 후에는 응답을 멈추어야 합니다. 이제 시작하겠습니다.

Q a: **What is your favorite food?**

Q b: **Where do you eat it?**

Q c: **Why do you like it?**

Q d: **How often do you eat it?**

| 1 | 2 | 3 | 4 |

OPEN NEAT

그림 묘사하기

차례

유형 미리 보기 – 그림 묘사하기

1 문제 보기 

국가영어능력평가시험

다음의 주어진 6개의 그림을 보고 그림에 적절한 이야기를 구성하여 말해 봅니다. 1분의 준비시간이 지나고 신호음이 들리면 1분 동안 답할 수 있습니다. 두 번의 짧은 신호음 후에는 응답을 멈추어야 합니다.

다음의 그림을 바탕으로 이야기를 영어로 구성해보세요. 이제 시작하겠습니다.

2 문제 풀이

① 소년이 잠에서 깨는 모습 – A boy gets up.
② 소년이 가족들과 아침 식사하는 모습 – Then he has breakfast with his family.
③ 소년이 학교 버스를 기다리는 모습 – He waits for the school bus.
④ 소년이 버스 의자에 앉는 모습 – He sits on the seat on the bus.
⑤ 소년이 친구와 얘기하는 모습 – And he talks to his friend.
⑥ 소년이 학교 버스에서 내리는 모습 – Finally, he gets off the bus at the school.

3 문제 파고 들기

① 그림 묘사하기란 어떤 문제인가요?

- 6개의 그림을 보고 순차적으로 이어지는 상황을 묘사하는 문제입니다.
- 대답을 준비할 시간이 1분 주어집니다.
- 1분 후 삐 소리가 한 번 나고, 대답할 시간이 1분 주어집니다.
- 1분 후 대답 종료를 알리는 두 번의 삐 소리가 나오면 대답을 멈춥니다.

② 그림 묘사하기에는 어떤 지시문이 나오나요?

- 다음의 그림을 바탕으로 이야기를 영어로 구성해 보세요.

4 문제 해결하기

① 그림을 보고 우선 누가, 언제, 어디에서, 무엇을 하는지에 대한 내용을 파악하세요.

- 예시문제에서는 한 소년이 아침에 일어나 학교에 도착하기까지의 과정을 그린 그림이 주어져 있습니다.

② 현재 시제, 현재 진행 시제, 과거 시제 등 이야기에 알맞은 시제 하나를 정해 일관성 있게 말하세요.

- A boy **gets** up. Then he **has** breakfast with his family.

③ 주어진 6개의 그림에 대한 각각의 내용을 빠짐없이 모두 묘사하세요.

- 잠에서 깨기 ⇨ 아침 식사하기 ⇨ 학교 버스 기다리기 ⇨ 버스 타기 ⇨ 친구와 얘기하기 ⇨ 버스에서 내리기

④ 앞 그림과 다음 그림 상황을 자연스럽게 연결하여 말할 수 있도록 연결 어구와 접속사를 많이 익혀 두세요.

- A boy gets up. **Then** he has breakfast with his family.
- He sits on the seat on the bus. **And** he talks to his friend.
- He talks to his friend. **Finally**, he gets off the bus at the school.

⑤ 평소에 여러 일상의 이야기들을 순서에 따라 말해보는 연습을 해보세요.

야외 활동

A 야외 활동과 관련된 표현을 익혀봅시다.

- 다음 표현을 듣고 큰소리로 따라 말해보세요.  08-02

run

play outside

make a snowman

go on a picnic

take a picture

camp out

go fishing

go shopping

eat out

B 야외 활동에 관한 표현을 현재 시제로 익혀봅시다.

- 주어가 3인칭 단수 (he, she, it, the boy 등)일 때 동사는 동사의 원형에 '-s', '-es', '-ies'가 붙거나 불규칙적으로 변화합니다.

- 다음 문장을 듣고 큰소리로 따라 말해보세요.  08-03

He / She runs.	**He / She** camps out.
He / She plays outside.	**He / She** goes fishing.
He / She makes a snowman.	**He / She** goes shopping.
He / She goes on a picnic.	**He / She** eats out.
He / She takes a picture.	

표현 연습

A 보기의 표현을 이용하여 그림 내용에 맞게 현재 시제로 문장을 완성하세요.

① 　②

③　④ 

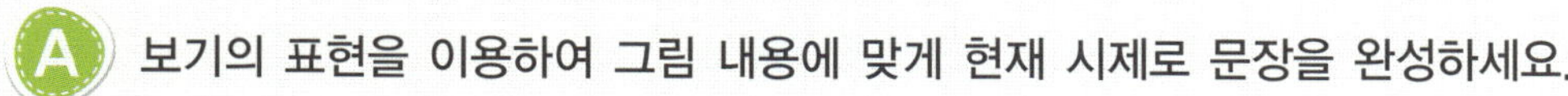

| play | run | go shopping | take a picture |

1. A woman ______________________ in the park.

2. A girl ______________________ .

3. A boy ______________________ with a ball.

4. A man ______________________ .

 필수 어휘　08-04

| **run** 달리다 | **go shopping** 쇼핑을 가다 | **take a picture** 사진을 찍다 |

B A번의 문장을 듣고 큰소리로 따라 말해보세요.　08-05

A 그림을 보고 주어진 표현을 이용하여 현재 시제로 문장을 완성하세요.

fly a kite　　　water the plants　　　make a snowman　　　take a picture

A boy _________________________ .

A girl _________________________ .

A boy _________________________ .

A girl _________________________ .

필수 어휘　🎧 08-06

fly a kite 연을 날리다　　　　　　　　**water the plants** 식물에 물을 주다
make a snowman 눈사람을 만들다　　　**take a picture** 사진을 찍다

B A번의 문장을 듣고 큰소리로 따라 말해보세요.　🎧 08-07

심화 말하기

A 그림을 보고 주어진 표현을 알맞게 배열하여 문장을 완성하세요.

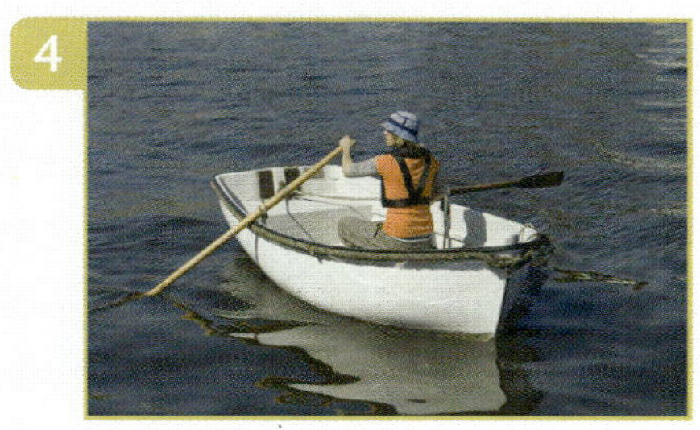

1. on the grass / . / with his dog / He runs

➡ ____

2. with his friend / . / badminton / A boy plays

➡ ____

3. basketball / on the court / . / A boy plays

➡ ____

4. in the lake / . / a boat / She rows

➡ ____

필수 어휘 🎧 08-08

along ~을 따라서   **play badminton** 배드민턴을 치다   **court** (테니스, 배구 등의) 코트
row 노를 젓다   **lake** 호수

B A번의 문장을 듣고 큰소리로 따라 말해보세요. 🎧 08-09

A 그림을 보고 보기에 주어진 표현을 이용하여 하나의 연결된 이야기를 현재 시제로 완성해보세요.

1  2  3 

4  5  6 

put on	throw the ball	walk towards
walk to the playground	stand	jump up

1. A boy ________________________ with his friend.

2. The two boys ________________________ their gloves.

3. And then the two boys ________________________ .

4. The boy ________________________ to his friend.

5. The boy's friend ________________________ to catch the ball.

6. Then the boy's friend ________________________ him.

필수 어휘  08-10

put on 입다, 쓰다	**throw** 던지다	**towards** ~쪽으로
stand 서있다	**jump up** 위로 뛰어오르다	**catch** 잡다

B A번의 문장을 듣고 큰소리로 따라 말해보세요.  08-11

C 그림을 보고 보기에 주어진 표현을 이용하여 하나의 연결된 이야기를 현재 시제로 완성해보세요.

1  2  3 

4  5  6 

walk along	say good bye	walk out of
on the swing	get home	buy

1. A boy _________________________ the school with a girl.

2. And they _________________________ hamburgers at a fast food restaurant.

3. And then they _________________________ the park and eat their hamburgers.

4. They play _________________________ .

5. Then the boy _________________________ to the girl.

6. Finally, the boy _________________________ .

 필수 어휘   08-12

walk along ~을 따라서 걷다   **say good bye** 작별인사를 하다   **walk out of** ~로부터 걸어나오다
swing 그네   **get home** 집에 오다   **buy** 사다

D C번의 문장을 듣고 큰소리로 따라 말해보세요.    08-13

 NEAT 실전 문제 유형을 풀어보세요.  08-14

국가영어능력평가시험

다음의 주어진 6개의 그림을 보고 그림에 적절한 이야기를 구성하여 말해 봅니다. 1분의 준비시간이 지나고 신호음이 들리면 1분 동안 답할 수 있습니다. 두 번의 짧은 신호음 후에는 응답을 멈추어야 합니다.

다음의 그림을 바탕으로 이야기를 영어로 구성해보세요. 이제 시작하겠습니다.

국가영어능력평가시험

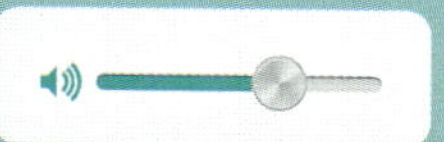

다음의 주어진 6개의 그림을 보고 그림에 적절한 이야기를 구성하여 말해 봅니다. 1분의 준비시간이 지나고 신호음이 들리면 1분 동안 답할 수 있습니다. 두 번의 짧은 신호음 후에는 응답을 멈추어야 합니다.

다음의 그림을 바탕으로 이야기를 영어로 구성해보세요. 이제 시작하겠습니다.

취미 / 오락 활동

A 취미, 오락 활동과 관련된 표현을 익혀봅시다.

● 다음 표현을 듣고 큰소리로 따라 말해보세요. 09-01

read a book

play baseball

sing a song

watch TV

see a movie

play the guitar

feed the birds

do a puzzle

play a board game

B 취미, 오락 활동에 관한 표현을 현재 시제로 익혀봅시다.

● 주어가 3인칭 단수 (he, she, it, the boy 등)일 때 동사는 동사의 원형에 '-s', '-es', '-ies'가 붙거나 또는 불규칙적으로 변화합니다.

● 다음의 문장을 듣고 큰소리로 따라 말해보세요. 09-02

He / She reads a book.	**He / She** plays the guitar.
He / She plays baseball.	**He / She** feeds the birds.
He / She sings a song.	**He / She** does a puzzle.
He / She watches TV.	**He / She** plays a board game.
He / She sees a movie.	

표현 연습

 **A** 보기의 표현을 이용하여 그림 내용에 맞게 현재 시제로 문장을 완성하세요.

1

2

3

4

| read | play | watch | feed |

1. A woman ______________________ TV.

2. A boy ______________________ the guitar.

3. A girl ______________________ the birds.

4. A boy ______________________ a book.

필수 어휘  09-03

play 연주하다　　　　feed 먹이를 주다　　　　guitar 기타

B A번의 문장을 듣고 큰소리로 따라 말해보세요.　09-04

기본 말하기

A 그림을 보고 주어진 표현을 이용하여 현재 시제로 문장을 완성하세요.

> sing a song   listen to music
> play the flute   play a computer game

A girl ________________________ .

A girl ________________________ .

A boy ________________________ .

A boy ________________________ .

필수 어휘   09-05

sing a song   노래를 부르다   listen to music   음악을 듣다
play the flute   플룻을 불다   play a computer game   컴퓨터 게임을 하다

B   A번의 문장을 듣고 큰소리로 따라 말해보세요.    09-06

심화 말하기

 **A** 그림을 보고 주어진 표현을 알맞게 배열하여 문장을 완성하세요.

1. a dog / . / feeds / A boy

➡ ______________________________________

2. the violin / . / He plays

➡ ______________________________________

3. tennis / . / A man plays

➡ ______________________________________

4. on the wall / . / darts / A boy plays

➡ ______________________________________

 필수 어휘　 09-07

feed 먹이를 주다	**play the violin** 바이올린을 연주하다
play tennis 테니스를 치다	**play darts** 다트 게임을 하다

B A번의 문장을 듣고 큰소리로 따라 말해보세요.  09-08

A 그림을 보고 보기에 주어진 표현을 이용하여 하나의 연결된 이야기를 현재 시제로 완성해보세요.

1  2  3 

4  5  6 

| pass a ball | sit on | walk out of |
| stand up | use a laptop computer | walk on |

1. A boy _________________________ the grass with a girl.

2. And they _________________________ the grass.

3. Then they _________________________ .

4. They _________________________ together.

5. And then the boy _________________________ to the girl.

6. Finally, they _________________________ the grass.

필수 어휘  09-09

pass a ball 공을 패스하다	walk out of ~로부터 걸어나오다
use a laptop computer 노트북을 사용하다	walk on ~ 위를 걷다

B A번의 문장을 듣고 큰소리로 따라 말해보세요.  09-10

C 그림을 보고 보기에 주어진 표현을 이용하여 하나의 연결된 이야기를 현재 시제로 완성해보세요.

1 
2 
3 

4 
5 
6 

merry-go-round	wait for	amusement park
roller coaster	ice cream	at the ticket booth

1. Two girls get to an ___________________________ .

2. They buy the tickets ___________________________ .

3. They ride a ___________________________ .

4. They eat ___________________________ .

5. They ___________________________ the roller coaster.

6. Then they enjoy the ___________________________ .

필수 어휘  09-11

merry-go-round 회전목마   **wait for** ~을 기다리다   **amusement park** 놀이공원
roller coaster 롤러코스터   **ticket booth** 매표소

D C번의 문장을 듣고 큰소리로 따라 말해보세요.  09-12

 NEAT 실전 문제 유형을 풀어보세요.  09-13

국가영어능력평가시험

다음의 주어진 6개의 그림을 보고 그림에 적절한 이야기를 구성하여 말해 봅니다. 1분의 준비시간이 지나고 신호음이 들리면 1분 동안 답할 수 있습니다. 두 번의 짧은 신호음 후에는 응답을 멈추어야 합니다.

다음의 그림을 바탕으로 이야기를 영어로 구성해보세요. 이제 시작하겠습니다.

1

2

3

4

5

6

1 2 3 4

국가영어능력평가시험 

다음의 주어진 6개의 그림을 보고 그림에 적절한 이야기를 구성하여 말해 봅니다. 1분의 준비시간이 지나고 신호음이 들리면 1분 동안 답할 수 있습니다. 두 번의 짧은 신호음 후에는 응답을 멈추어야 합니다.

다음의 그림을 바탕으로 이야기를 영어로 구성해보세요. 이제 시작하겠습니다.

1

2

3

4

5

6

Unit 10

개인 / 단체 활동

A 개인, 단체 활동과 관련된 표현을 익혀봅시다.

● 다음 표현을 듣고 큰소리로 따라 말해보세요.  10-01

watch a movie

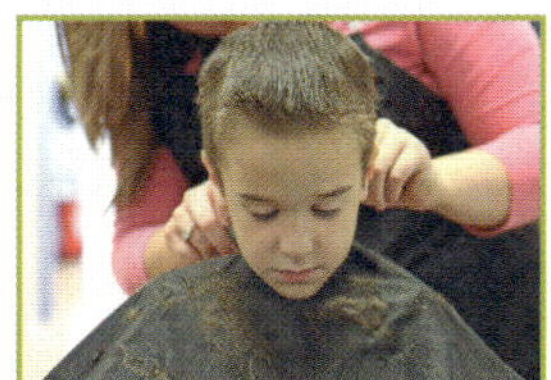
get a haircut

write an email

take a nap

visit a museum

write in a diary

dance with

have a meeting

sing in a chorus

B 개인, 단체 활동에 관한 표현을 현재 시제로 익혀봅시다.

● 주어가 3인칭 단수 (he, she, it, the boy 등)일 때 동사는 동사의 원형에 '-s', '-es', '-ies'가 붙거나 또는 불규칙적으로 변화합니다.

● 다음 문장을 듣고 큰소리로 따라 말해보세요.  10-02

He / She watch**es** a movie.	**He / She** write**s** in a diary.
He / She get**s** a haircut.	**He / She** dance**s** with friends.
He / She write**s** an email.	**He / She has** a meeting.
He / She take**s** a nap.	**He / She** sing**s** in a chorus.
He / She goe**s** to a museum.	

 표현 연습

A 보기의 표현을 이용하여 그림 내용에 맞게 현재 시제로 문장을 완성하세요.

1

2

3

4

| work | sing in a chorus | write in a diary | watch a movie |

1. He _____________________ with his classmates.

2. The girl _____________________ .

3. A boy _____________________ with a friend.

4. A boy _____________________ with his friend on the farm.

필수 어휘  10-03

sing in a chorus 합창하다   **write in a diary** 일기를 쓰다   **watch a movie** 영화를 보다
classmate 같은 반 친구   **farm** 농장

B A번의 문장을 듣고 큰소리로 따라 말해보세요.  10-04

A 그림을 보고 주어진 표현을 이용하여 현재 시제로 문장을 완성하세요.

is in the museum	work with dad
have a meeting	get up in the morning

A boy ___________________ .

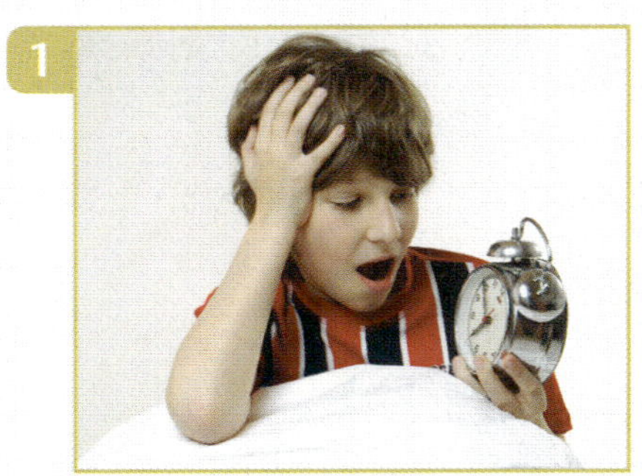

A girl ___________________ .

A boy ___________________ .

A woman ___________________ .

 10-05

museum 박물관
have a meeting 회의가 있다

work with ~와 함께 일하다
get up in the morning 아침에 일어나다

B A번의 문장을 듣고 큰소리로 따라 말해보세요. 10-06

심화 말하기

 그림을 보고 주어진 표현을 알맞게 배열하여 문장을 완성하세요.

1. a girl / . / He smiles at

➡ ____

2. in the meeting / . / She is

➡ ____

3. in the restaurant / . / a meal / A boy eats

➡ ____

4. A girl / . / a haircut / gets

➡ ____

필수 어휘　🎧 10-07

smile at ~를 보고 웃다　　　　**meal** 식사　　　　**get a haircut** 머리를 자르다

B A번의 문장을 듣고 큰소리로 따라 말해보세요.　🎧 10-08

A 그림을 보고 보기에 주어진 표현을 이용하여 하나의 연결된 이야기를 현재 시제로 완성해보세요.

1 
2 
3 

4 
5 
6 

| walk to | watch | read |
| yawn | get up | sleep |

1. A boy _________________________ TV on the sofa.

2. He _________________________ from the sofa.

3. He _________________________ his room.

4. He _________________________ a book at the desk.

5. He _________________________ .

6. Then he _________________________ on the bed.

필수 어휘  10-09

walk to ~로 걸어가다　　　**yawn** 하품하다　　　**then** 그리고 나서

B A번의 문장을 듣고 큰소리로 따라 말해보세요.  10-10

C 그림을 보고 보기에 주어진 표현을 이용하여 하나의 연결된 이야기를 현재 시제로 완성해보세요.

1    2    3 

4    5    6 

the poor girls	talk to	give presents
sweep the street	help	pick up

1. Three girls ________________________ each other.

2. They ________________________ the trash.

3. They ________________________ near the house.

4. Then they play with ________________________ .

5. They ________________________ the poor girls eat lunch.

6. They ________________________ to the poor girls.

필수 어휘  10-11

poor 불우한	**give presents** 선물을 주다	**sweep** 빗자루로 쓸다
pick up 줍다	**each other** 서로	**trash** 쓰레기

D C번의 문장을 듣고 큰소리로 따라 말해보세요.  10-12

 NEAT 실전 문제 유형을 풀어보세요.  

국가영어능력평가시험

다음의 주어진 6개의 그림을 보고 그림에 적절한 이야기를 구성하여 말해 봅니다. 1분의 준비시간이 지나고 신호음이 들리면 1분 동안 답할 수 있습니다. 두 번의 짧은 신호음 후에는 응답을 멈추어야 합니다.

다음의 그림을 바탕으로 이야기를 영어로 구성해보세요. 이제 시작하겠습니다.

1

2

3

4

5

6

1 2 3 4

국가영어능력평가시험 

다음의 주어진 6개의 그림을 보고 그림에 적절한 이야기를 구성하여 말해 봅니다. 1분의 준비시간이 지나고 신호음이 들리면 1분 동안 답할 수 있습니다. 두 번의 짧은 신호음 후에는 응답을 멈추어야 합니다.

다음의 그림을 바탕으로 이야기를 영어로 구성해보세요. 이제 시작하겠습니다.

1

2

3

4

5

6

문제 해결하기

차례

유형 미리 보기 – 문제 해결하기

1 문제 보기 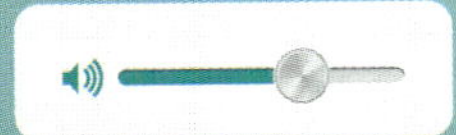

다음은 어떤 문제나 상황을 묘사하고 있습니다. 이 문제나 상황을 어떻게 해결할 것인가를 1분 동안 생각하세요. 신호음이 울리면 1분 동안 답할 수 있습니다. 두 번의 짧은 신호음 후에는 응답을 멈춰야 합니다. 이제 시작하겠습니다.

You will go swimming with your friend at 2 p.m. It's already 2 p.m. and your friend is waiting for you. But your mom is asking you to wash the dishes now. What would you like to say to your mom?

2 문제 풀이

- 문제 풀이: 친구와 먼저 2시에 만나기로 약속을 했고, 친구가 나를 기다리는 상황이므로 어머니께 수영에서 돌아온 뒤에 도와드리겠다고 정중히 양해를 구하는 말을 하도록 합니다.

- 모범 답안: Mom, I am afraid I can't. I planned to go swimming with my friend and my friend is waiting for me now. I don't want to be late. I'll help you after I come back home. Sorry, mom.

- 해석: 엄마, 죄송하지만 안될 것 같아요. 친구랑 수영가기로 했고, 지금 친구가 저를 기다리고 있어요. 늦고 싶지 않아요. 집에 돌아와서 도와 드릴게요. 죄송해요, 엄마.

3 문제 파고 들기

① 문제 해결하기란 어떤 문제인가요?

- 다소 긴 지문의 일상 생활 관련 상황이 주어지면 그것을 어떻게 해결할 것인지 나 자신의 생각과 의견을 조리 있게 말하는 문제입니다.
- 문제는 화면에 제시되며 또한 음성으로도 주어집니다.
- 문제가 주어진 후 응답을 준비하는 시간은 1분입니다.
- 삐 소리를 듣고 난 후 대답할 시간은 1분입니다.
- 두 번의 짧은 삐 소리가 나오면 대답을 멈추어야 합니다.

② 문제 해결하기에는 어떤 상황들이 주어지나요?

- 양해를 구하며 거절하기
- 친구에게 충고하기
- 나의 의견을 제안하기
- 다른 이에게 부탁하기

4 문제 해결하기

① 다소 긴 글을 읽고 들으며 문제를 정해진 시간 내에 파악해야 하므로 주어진 핵심 내용을 빠르게 파악하는 능력이 필요합니다.

② 문제가 되는 상황을 정확히 파악한 다음, 우선 상황을 간단히 정리하여 설명한 후 어떤 해결책을 제시할 것인지 내용을 구성하세요.

③ 문제 해결에 필요하고 상황에 맞는 다양한 표현을 많이 익혀두세요. 양해를 구하는 상황, 충고하는 상황, 제안하는 상황, 부탁하는 상황, 거절하는 상황 등 여러 상황이 주어지므로 평소에 다양한 표현을 알아두는 것이 중요합니다.

④ 좋은 평가를 받기 위한 핵심은 '주어진 상황에 대한 적절한 해결책을, 주어진 시간 안에 답하는 것'입니다. 따라서 다양한 상황을 해결하는 영어 표현 능력과 더불어 이 유형에 익숙해지도록 많은 연습을 해보세요.

중요 표현 익히기

A 정중히 거절하는 표현을 익혀봅시다.

● 다음 표현을 듣고 큰소리로 따라 말해보세요. **11-02**

• I'm sorry, but I can't.	미안하지만 안될 것 같아요.
• I am afraid I can't.	미안하지만 안될 것 같아요.
• I'd love to ~, but I can't.	나도 ~하고 싶지만 안될 것 같아요.
• I'd like to ~, but I can't.	나도 ~하고 싶지만 안될 것 같아요.

표현 연습

A 주어진 보기의 표현을 모두 사용하여 정중히 거절하는 표현을 완성해보세요.

1.	• I'm sorry, but I can't. • I am afraid I can't.	______________________ I am busy now.
2.	• I am afraid I can't. • I'd love to, but I can't.	______________________ I have to go home now.
3.	• I'd love to, but I can't. • I'd like to, but I can't.	______________________ I don't have time now.

필수 어휘 **11-03**

busy 바쁜   have to ~해야 한다   now 지금

B A번의 문장을 듣고 큰소리로 따라 말해보세요. **11-04**

C 그림을 보고 주어진 표현을 사용하여 문장을 완성하세요. 한 문제에 답이 두 개 이상이 될 수 있습니다.

1	2	3	4

I am sorry   I am afraid   I'd love to   I'd like to

1. **A**: Would you like some coffee?

   B: _____________________ I can't. I don't like coffee.

2. **A**: Do you want to play a computer game with me?

   B: _____________________, but I can't. I am busy now.

3. **A**: How about playing badminton together?

   B: _____________________, but I can't. I have to go back home.

4. **A**: Would you like to skate together?

   B: _____________________, but I can't. I have a headache.

필수 어휘 🎧 11-05

play a computer game 컴퓨터 게임을 하다 **go back home** 집에 돌아가다
skate 스케이트 타다 **have a headache** 두통이 있다

D C번의 대화를 듣고 큰소리로 따라 말해보세요. 🎧 11-06

A 문제를 해결하기 위한 단계별 답안을 작성해봅시다. 주어진 표현을 알맞게 배열하여 문장을 완성해보세요.

> Your friend asks you to play soccer together. But you have to go home and take care of your baby sister. What would you like to say to your friend?
>
> 당신의 친구가 함께 축구를 하자고 말합니다. 하지만 당신은 집에 가서 아기 여동생을 돌봐줘야 합니다. 친구에게 뭐라고 말하겠습니까?

1. **거절의 표현**: 나도 그러고 싶지만 안될 것 같아.

   ① ____

   I can't / I'd love / but / to / . / ,

2. **거절의 이유**: 나 지금 집에 가야 해. 아기 여동생을 돌봐야 하거든.

   ② ____

   . / go home / I / have to / now

   ③ ____

   I / my baby sister / . / take care of / need to

3. **문제 해결의 마무리**: 미안해. 하지만 나 내일은 축구 할 수 있어.

   ④ ____

   sorry / I / am / .

   ⑤ ____

   tomorrow / I can / . / play soccer / But

필수 어휘 🎧 11-07

ask 묻다   **take care of** ~을 돌보다   **baby sister** 아기 여동생   **need to** ~을 해야 한다

B A번의 문장을 듣고 큰소리로 따라 말해보세요. 🎧 11-08

 심화 말하기

A 문제를 해결하기 위한 단계별 답안을 작성해봅시다. 빈칸에 들어갈 알맞은 말을 보기에서 찾아 문장을 완성해보세요.

You're playing with your best friend. It's time to go home. But your friend wants to play more with you. You promised your mom you'd get back home by 6 o'clock. What would you say to your friend?

So I need to	to play with you more	by 6 o'clock
promised my mom	go home now	sorry

1. 거절의 표현: 미안하지만 안될 것 같아.

① I'm ＿＿＿＿＿＿＿＿＿＿＿＿ , but I can't.

2. 거절의 이유: 너와 더 놀고 싶지만 나는 지금 집에 가야 해. 엄마에게 6시까지 집에 가겠다고 약속했어.

② I want ＿＿＿＿＿＿＿＿＿＿ , but I have to ＿＿＿＿＿＿＿＿＿＿ .

③ I ＿＿＿＿＿＿＿＿＿＿ I'd get back home ＿＿＿＿＿＿＿＿＿＿ .

3. 문제 해결의 마무리: 그래서 나 지금 집에 가야 돼. 미안해.

④ ＿＿＿＿＿＿＿＿＿＿ get back home now. I'm sorry.

 필수 어휘 11-09

best friend 가장 친한 친구	**It's time to ~.** ~할 시간이다.	**more** 더 많이
promised 약속했다	**get back home** 집에 돌아가다	**by** ~까지

B A번의 문장을 듣고 큰소리로 따라 말해보세요.  11-10

실전 유형 대비하기

A 다음은 어떤 문제나 상황을 묘사하고 있습니다. 주어진 표현을 알맞게 배열하여 문장을 완성해 보세요.

> You want to go to a movie today. There is a good movie in the theater. You want to see that movie today. But your friend wants to play outside with you. What would you like to say to him?

1. 거절의 표현

① ____

. / I'd like to / but I can't / ,

2. 거절의 이유

② ____

go to a movie / today / I want to / .

③ ____

in the theater / There is / . / a good movie

3. 문제 해결의 마무리

④ ____

. / next time / play outside / Let's

필수 어휘 11-11

go to a movie 영화 보러 가다	**theater** 극장	**play outside** 밖에서 놀다
Let's ~. ~하자.	**next time** 다음번에	

B A번의 문장을 듣고 큰소리로 따라 말해보세요. 11-12

C 다음은 어떤 문제나 상황을 묘사하고 있습니다. 주어진 표현을 알맞게 배열하여 문장을 완성해 보세요.

> You have a cold and you feel sleepy. You want to rest. But your friend calls you. She wants to have lunch outside with you. What would you like to say to your friend?

1. 거절의 표현

① ____

I'd love to / . / , / I can't / but

2. 거절의 이유

② ____

I have a cold / I feel sleepy / . / and

③ ____

. / I want to / rest

3. 문제 해결의 마무리

④ ____

go outside / . / So / I can't

필수 어휘 🎧 11-13

have a cold 감기에 걸리다	**feel sleepy** 졸리다	**rest** 쉬다
call 전화하다	**go outside** 외출하다	

D C번의 문장을 듣고 큰소리로 따라 말해보세요. 🎧 11-14

 NEAT 실전 문제 유형을 풀어보세요.  11-15

국가영어능력평가시험 

다음은 어떤 문제나 상황을 묘사하고 있습니다. 이 문제나 상황을 어떻게 해결할 것인가를 1분 동안 생각하세요. 신호음이 울리면 1분 동안 답할 수 있습니다. 두 번의 짧은 신호음 후에는 응답을 멈춰야 합니다. 이제 시작하겠습니다.

You and your friends are going to play baseball this afternoon. But your mother wants to go shopping with you. You can't go shopping with your mother because of the baseball game. What would you say to your mother?

1 2 3 4

국가영어능력평가시험

다음은 어떤 문제나 상황을 묘사하고 있습니다. 이 문제나 상황을 어떻게 해결할 것인가를 1분 동안 생각하세요. 신호음이 울리면 1분 동안 답할 수 있습니다. 두 번의 짧은 신호음 후에는 응답을 멈춰야 합니다. 이제 시작하겠습니다.

You are in the library. You are reading a book. It is interesting. Your friend asks you to go out to eat something. But you want to finish this book. What would you like to say to your friend?

Unit 12 — 부탁하기

A 정중히 부탁하는 표현을 익혀봅시다.

- Would you ~?   ~을 해주시겠어요?
- May I ~?   제가 ~을 해도 될까요?
- Could you ~?   ~을 해주시겠어요?
- Could I ~?   제가 ~을 해도 될까요?

표현 연습

A 주어진 표현을 모두 사용하여 정중히 부탁하는 표현을 완성해보세요.

1.	• Would you lift this box for me? • Could you lift this box for me?	________________ This box is too heavy for me.
2.	• Would you open the door for me? • Could you open the door for me?	________________ I have too many books in my hands.
3.	• May I borrow your pencil? • Could I borrow your pencil?	________________ I can't find my pencil.
4.	• May I use your eraser? • Could I use your eraser?	________________ I don't have one.

필수 어휘   12-01

lift 들어올리다	**too heavy** 너무 무거운	**too many** 너무 많은
borrow 빌리다	**eraser** 지우개	**one** (어떤) 것

B A번의 문장을 듣고 큰소리로 따라 말해보세요.    12-02

C 그림을 보고 주어진 표현을 사용하여 문장을 완성하세요. 한 문제에 답이 두 개 이상이 될 수 있습니다.

1   2   3   4

Would you   Could you   May I   Could I

1. **A:** _____________________ say that one more time?

   B: No problem.

2. **A:** _____________________ give me some water?

   B: Certainly.

3. **A:** _____________________ sit here?

   B: Yes, of course.

4. **A:** _____________________ join your soccer game?

   B: Sure.

필수 어휘 🎧 12-03		
one more time 한번 더	**No problem.** 물론이죠.	**Certainly.** 물론이죠.
Of course. 물론이죠.	**join** 함께 하다	**Sure.** 물론이죠.

D C번의 대화를 듣고 큰소리로 따라 말해보세요.  🎧 12-04

A 문제를 해결하기 위한 단계별 답안을 작성해봅시다. 빈칸에 들어갈 알맞은 말을 보기에서 찾아 문장을 완성해보세요.

> You are in the library. You are looking for the book, "The History of Korea." But you can't find it. Then you see a librarian at the information desk. What would you like to say to the man?
>
> 당신은 도서관에 있습니다. 당신은 "한국의 역사"라는 책을 찾고 있습니다. 하지만 그것을 찾을 수가 없습니다. 그 때 당신은 안내 데스크에서 도서관 직원을 봅니다. 당신은 그 남자에게 뭐라고 말하겠습니까?

Would you help me	how are you
looking for	can't find it

1. **인사말:** 안녕하세요?

   ① Hi, _________________________ ?

2. **상황 설명:** 저는 "한국의 역사"라는 책을 찾고 있는데 이 구역에서 찾을 수가 없네요.

   ② I am _________________________ the book, "The History of Korea."

   ③ But I _________________________ in this section.

3. **부탁의 표현:** 제가 책을 찾는 것을 도와주시겠어요?

   ④ _________________________ find the book?

필수 어휘 12-05

library 도서관	look for ~을 찾다	find 발견하다
librarian (도서관의) 사서	information desk 안내 데스크	section 구역

B A번의 문장을 듣고 큰소리로 따라 말해보세요. 12-06

심화 말하기

A 문제를 해결하기 위한 단계별 답안을 작성해봅시다. 주어진 표현을 알맞게 배열하여 문장을 완성해보세요.

> You are doing your math homework. But it is too difficult. You need someone's help. You can ask your mother to help you. What would you like to say to your mother?

1. **부탁의 표현:** 이 문제 푸는 것을 도와주실래요?

   ① ____

   ? / help me / Would you / solve this question

2. **부탁의 이유:** 이 문제는 너무 어려워요. 그래서 풀 수가 없어요.

   ② ____

   too difficult / is / This question / .

   ③ ____

   it / . / can't solve / I / So

3. **문제 해결의 마무리:** 제 숙제를 도와주시겠어요?

   ④ ____

   help me / Would you / with my homework / ?

필수 어휘  12-07

math homework 수학 숙제	**too difficult** 너무 어려운
someone's help 누군가의 도움	**solve** 문제를 풀다

B A번의 문장을 듣고 큰소리로 따라 말해보세요.  12-08

A 다음은 어떤 문제나 상황을 묘사하고 있습니다. 주어진 표현을 알맞게 배열하여 문장을 완성해보세요.

> You are studying. You are hungry. You want to eat something but your mother, is watching TV. What would you like to say to your mother?

1. 상황 설명

   ① ____

   . / I am hungry / I'm sorry mom / but / ,

2. 부탁의 표현

   ② ____

   make me / ? / Would you / some food

   ③ ____

   something / eat / I want to / .

3. 문제 해결의 마무리

   ④ ____

   very much / Thank you / .

필수 어휘 12-09

hungry 배고픈   Would you ~? ~해주시겠어요?   something 무언가

B A번의 문장을 듣고 큰소리로 따라 말해보세요. 12-10

C 다음은 어떤 문제나 상황을 묘사하고 있습니다. 주어진 표현을 알맞게 배열하여 문장을 완성해보세요.

> You are studying. You have an English word test tomorrow. You want to eat ice cream, but you can't go out because you are busy. Your brother will go to a supermarket to buy something. What would you like to say to your brother?

1. 부탁의 표현

① ________________________________ at the supermarket?

buy me / Would you / ice cream

2. 부탁의 이유

② I am studying because ________________________________ .

tomorrow / I have / an English word test

③ ________________________________

now / . / I am / So / busy

3. 문제 해결의 마무리

④ ________________________________

! / so much / Thank you

필수 어휘 🎧 12-11

English word test 영어 단어 테스트　　　　**go out** 외출하다　　　　**busy** 바쁜

D C번의 문장을 듣고 큰소리로 따라 말해보세요. 🎧 12-12

 NEAT 실전 문제 유형을 풀어보세요.  12-13

국가영어능력평가시험 

다음은 어떤 문제나 상황을 묘사하고 있습니다. 이 문제나 상황을 어떻게 해결할 것인가를 1분 동안 생각하세요. 신호음이 울리면 1분 동안 답할 수 있습니다. 두 번의 짧은 신호음 후에는 응답을 멈춰야 합니다. 이제 시작하겠습니다.

You have a computer. It is old. Sometimes it doesn't work well. You want to buy a new one. You can ask your mother to buy a new computer. What would you like to say to your mother?

1 2 3 4

국가영어능력평가시험

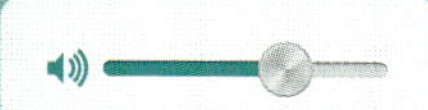

다음은 어떤 문제나 상황을 묘사하고 있습니다. 이 문제나 상황을 어떻게 해결할 것인가를 1분 동안 생각하세요. 신호음이 울리면 1분 동안 답할 수 있습니다. 두 번의 짧은 신호음 후에는 응답을 멈춰야 합니다. 이제 시작하겠습니다.

It's raining. You don't have an umbrella with you. You can't go home because of heavy rain. Nobody has an umbrella around you. You want to ask your mother to bring an umbrella. What would you like to say to your mother?

1 2 3 4

OPEN NEAT

SPEAKING Level 1

실전 유형 평가

실전 유형 평가

1 그림 보고 질문에 답하기 🎧 13-01

다음의 제시된 그림을 보고 질문에 한 두 개의 완전한 문장으로 답하세요. 10초의 준비시간이 지나고 신호음이 들리면 15초 동안 답할 수 있습니다. 두 번의 짧은 신호음 후에는 응답을 멈춰야 합니다. 이제 시작하겠습니다.

Q a: What is the boy doing?

Q b: Is the girl happy?

Q c: Where are they?

2 연계 질문에 답하기  13-02

당신은 오늘 오후에 친구와 점심 식사를 할 것입니다. 당신의 친구가 당신에게 다음 네 가지 질문을 합니다. 친구의 질문에 각각 한 두 개의 완전한 영어 문장으로 답하세요. 각 문항 당 10초의 준비시간이 지나고 신호음이 들리면 15초 동안 답할 수 있습니다. 두 번의 짧은 신호음 후에는 응답을 멈춰야 합니다. 이제 시작하겠습니다.

> **Q a: What time shall we meet?**
>
> **Q b: What would you like for lunch?**
>
> **Q c: Why do you like it?**
>
> **Q d: Where shall we go?**

3 그림 묘사하기 🎧 13-03

다음의 주어진 6개의 그림을 보고 그림에 적절한 이야기를 구성하여 말해 봅니다. 1분의 준비 시간이 지나고 신호음이 들리면 1분 동안 답할 수 있습니다. 두 번의 짧은 신호음 후에는 응답을 멈춰야 합니다.

다음의 그림을 바탕으로 이야기를 영어로 구성해 보세요. 이제 시작하겠습니다.

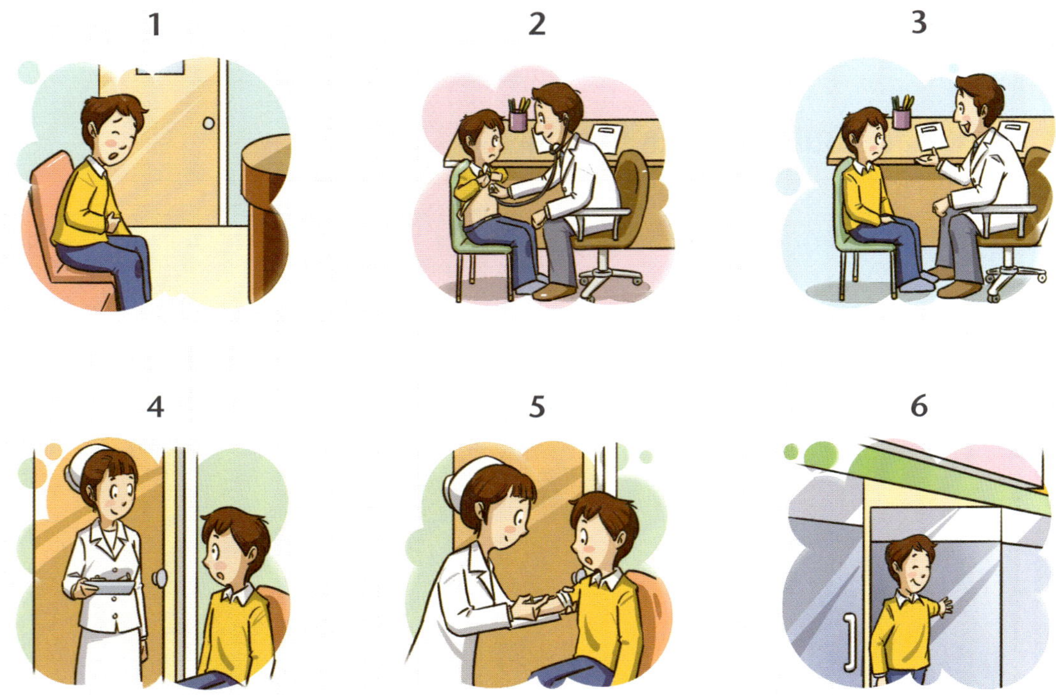

4 문제 해결하기  13-04

다음은 어떤 문제나 상황을 묘사하고 있습니다. 이 문제나 상황을 어떻게 해결할 것인가를 1분 동안 생각하세요. 신호음이 울리면 1분 동안 답할 수 있습니다. 두 번의 짧은 신호음 후에는 응답을 멈춰야 합니다. 이제 시작하겠습니다.

One of your friends asks you to go to the movies tonight. But you already have an appointment. You and your mom will go to a concert. So you can't go see a movie with your friend. What would you say to your friend?

MEMO

OPEN NEAT

National English Ability Test

SPEAKING

Level 1

정답 및 해석

Part 1 그림 보고 질문에 답하기

Unit 01 그림 속 동작 묘사하기

표현 연습 p.15

A 1. is cooking   2. are reading
     3. are talking   4. are sitting

A

1. A woman is cooking in the kitchen.
한 여자가 부엌에서 요리를 하고 있다.

2. They are reading books at the desk.
그들은 책상에서 책을 읽고 있다.

3. A boy and a girl are talking to each other.
한 소년과 한 소녀가 서로 이야기를 하고 있다.

4. People are sitting on the grass.
사람들이 잔디 위에 앉아 있다.

기본 말하기 p.16

A 1. watching TV, talking on the phone
     2. jumping, hitting a ball
     3. drinking orange juice, cooking spaghetti
     4. writing his name, reading a book

A

1. The man is watching TV.
The man is not talking on the phone.

그 남자는 TV를 보고 있다.
그 남자는 전화 통화를 하고 있지 않다.

2. They are jumping.
They are not hitting a ball.

그들은 점프하고 있다.
그들은 공을 치고 있지 않다.

3. She is drinking orange juice.
She is not cooking spaghetti.

그녀는 오렌지 주스를 마시고 있다.
그녀는 스파게티를 요리하고 있지 않다.

4. The boy is writing his name.
The boy is not reading a book.

그 소년은 자신의 이름을 쓰고 있다.
그 소년은 책을 읽고 있지 않다.

심화 말하기 p.17

A 1. is drinking   2. is eating   3. is watching
     4. is carrying   5. is reading

A

1. The old man is drinking coffee.
그 노인은 커피를 마시고 있다.

2. The man is eating fruit.
그 남자는 과일을 먹고 있다.

3. The boy is watching TV.
그 소년은 TV를 보고 있다.

4. The woman is carrying some food.
그 여자는 약간의 음식을 나르고 있다.

5. The girl is reading a magazine.
그 소녀는 잡지책을 읽고 있다.

실전 유형 대비하기 pp.18-19

A 1. No, is throwing a ball
     2. No, are running
     3. Yes, is drinking juice

C **1.** is playing the piano

2. are getting on the bus

3. are eating spaghetti

A

1. Q: Is the boy catching a ball?

   A: <u>No</u>, he isn't. He <u>is throwing a ball</u>.

   Q: 그 소년은 공을 잡고 있나요?

   A: 아니요. 그는 공을 던지고 있어요.

2. Q: Are they walking?

   A: <u>No</u>, they aren't. They <u>are running</u>.

   Q: 그들은 걷고 있나요?

   A: 아니요. 그들은 달리고 있어요.

3. Q: Is the boy drinking something?

   A: <u>Yes</u>, he is. He <u>is drinking juice</u>.

   Q: 그 소년이 뭔가를 마시고 있나요?

   A: 네. 그는 주스를 마시고 있어요.

C

1. Q: What is the girl doing?

   A: She <u>is playing the piano</u>.

   Q: 그 소녀는 무엇을 하고 있나요?

   A: 그녀는 피아노를 치고 있어요.

2. Q: What are they doing?

   A: They <u>are getting on the bus</u>.

   Q: 그들은 무엇을 하고 있나요?

   A: 그들은 버스를 타고 있어요.

3. Q: What are the people eating?

   A: They <u>are eating spaghetti</u> in the restaurant.

   Q: 그 사람들은 무엇을 먹고 있나요?

   A: 그들은 식당에서 스파게티를 먹고 있어요.

단원 평가 pp.20-21

A

Q a: What is the girl doing?

그 소녀는 무엇을 하고 있나요?

모범 답안 She is writing an email.

그녀는 이메일을 쓰고 있어요.

필수 어휘

writing 쓰고 있는 / email 이메일

해설

그림 속 소녀가 무엇을 하고 있는지를 묘사해야 하는 문제이므로 우선 소녀가 무엇을 보고 있고, 무엇을 하고 있는지를 파악해야 합니다. 소녀가 눈으로 보고 있는 것은 컴퓨터 화면 속 이메일 창이고, 손은 키보드의 타자를 치는 것을 보아 소녀는 이메일을 쓰고 있으므로 이를 현재 진행 시제인 'She / is writing / an email.'이라고 말하세요.

Q b: Are they standing on the grass?

그들은 잔디 위에 서 있나요?

모범 답안 No, they aren't. They are sitting on the grass.

아니요. 그들은 잔디 위에 앉아 있어요.

필수 어휘

standing 서있는 / on the grass 잔디 위에 /
sitting 앉아 있는

해설

두 소녀가 잔디 위에 앉아 있으므로 '그들이 잔디 위에 서있나요?'라는 be동사 Yes / No 의문문에 일단 '아니요, 그렇지 않습니다.' 즉, 'No, they aren't.'라고 말합니다. 그리고 나서 '그들은 앉아 있어요.'라는 내용을 현재 진행 시제인 'They / are sitting / on the grass.'라고 말하세요.

Q c: Is the boy reading a newspaper?

그 소년은 신문을 읽고 있나요?

모범 답안 No, he isn't. He is watching TV.

아니요. 그는 TV를 보고 있어요.

필수 어휘

reading 읽고 있는 / newspaper 신문 /
watching 보고 있는

소년이 신문을 보는 것이 아니라 TV를 보고 있으므로 '소년은 신문을 읽고 있나요?'라는 be동사 Yes/No 의문문에 일단 '아니요, 그렇지 않습니다.' 즉, 'No, he isn't.'라고 말합니다. 그리고 나서 '소년은 TV를 보고 있어요.'라는 내용을 현재 진행 시제인 'They / are sitting / on the grass.'라고 말하세요.

B

Q a: What is the girl doing?

그 소녀는 무엇을 하고 있나요?

모범 답안 She is reading a comic book.

그녀는 만화책을 읽고 있어요.

필수 어휘

reading 읽고 있는 / comic book 만화책

해설

그림 속 소녀가 무엇을 하고 있는지를 묘사해야 하는 문제이므로 우선 소녀가 무엇을 보고 있고, 무엇을 하고 있는지를 파악해야 합니다. 소녀가 보고 있는 것은 책인데 표지에 만화 그림이 있고 소녀가 깔깔 웃는 것으로 보아 만화책을 읽고 있으므로 이를 현재 진행 시제인 'She / is reading / a comic book.'이라고 말하세요.

Q b: What are the boys doing?

그 소년들은 무엇을 하고 있나요?

모범 답안 They are playing soccer in the playground.

그들은 운동장에서 축구를 하고 있어요.

필수 어휘

playing soccer 축구를 하고 있는 /
in the playground 운동장에서

해설

그림 속 소년들이 무엇을 하고 있는지를 묘사해야 하는 문제이므로 우선 소년들이 무엇을 보고 있고, 무엇을 하고 있는지를 파악해야 합니다. 장소는 운동장이고 그들이 보고 있는 것은 축구공이며 서로 공을 차는 것으로 보아 축구를 하고 있습니다. 이 내용을 현재 진행 시제인 'They / are playing soccer / in the playground.'라고 말하세요.

Q c: Is the boy eating fruit?

그 소년은 과일을 먹고 있나요?

모범 답안 No, he isn't. He is eating ice cream.

아니요. 그는 아이스크림을 먹고 있어요.

필수 어휘

eating 먹고 있는 / fruit 과일 / ice cream 아이스크림

해설

소년은 과일이 아니라 아이스크림을 먹고 있으므로 '소년은 과일을 먹고 있나요?'라는 be동사 Yes/No 의문문에 일단 '아니요, 그렇지 않습니다.' 즉, 'No, he isn't.'라고 말합니다. 그리고 나서 '그는 아이스크림을 먹고 있어요.'라는 내용을 현재 진행 시제인 'He / is eating / ice cream.'이라고 말하세요.

Unit 02 그림 속 상태 묘사하기

표현 연습 p.23

A 1. cold 2. kind
   3. dirty 4. delicious

A

1. The weather is very <u>cold</u>.
   날씨가 매우 춥다.

2. The girl is so <u>kind</u>.
   그 소녀는 매우 친절하다.

3. The hands are too <u>dirty</u>.
   그 손은 너무 더럽다.

4. The food is <u>delicious</u>.
   그 음식은 맛있다.

기본 말하기 p.24

A 1. interesting, boring
   2. warm, cold
   3. kind, rude
   4. clean, dirty

A

1. The game is <u>interesting</u>.
   The game is not <u>boring</u>.

   그 게임은 재미있다.
   그 게임은 지루하지 않다.

2. It is <u>warm</u>.
   It is not <u>cold</u>.

   날씨가 따뜻하다.
   날씨가 춥지 않다.

3. The boy is <u>kind</u>.
   The boy is not <u>rude</u>.

   그 소년은 친절하다.
   그 소년은 버릇 없지 않다.

4. The room is <u>clean</u>.
   The room is not <u>dirty</u>.

   그 방은 깨끗하다.
   그 방은 더럽지 않다.

심화 말하기　　　　　　　　　　p.25

| **A** 1. windy | 2. rude | 3. kind |
| 4. sleepy | 5. pretty | |

A

1. It is <u>windy</u> today.
   오늘은 바람이 많이 분다.

2. The boy is <u>rude</u>.
   그 소년은 무례하다.

3. The girl is <u>kind</u>.
   그 소녀는 친절하다.

4. The boy is <u>sleepy</u>.
   그 소년은 졸린다.

5. Her dress is <u>pretty</u>.
   그녀의 드레스는 예쁘다.

실전 유형 대비하기　　　　　　　pp.26-27

A 1. Yes, is tired	2. No, is happy
3. No, is cold	
C 1. is exciting	2. is sunny and hot
3. looks healthy	

A

1. Q: Is the boy tired?
   A: <u>Yes</u>, he <u>is tired</u>.

   Q: 그 소년은 지쳤나요?
   A: 네, 그는 지쳤어요.

2. Q: Is the girl sad?
   A: <u>No</u>, she isn't. She <u>is happy</u>.

   Q: 그 소녀는 슬픈가요?
   A: 아니요. 그녀는 행복해요.

3. Q: Is it warm outside?
   A: <u>No</u>, it isn't. It <u>is cold</u> outside.

   Q: 바깥 날씨가 따뜻한가요?
   A: 아니요. 밖에는 추워요.

C

1. Q: How is the concert?
   A: The concert <u>is exciting</u>.

   Q: 그 콘서트는 어떤가요?
   A: 그 콘서트는 신나요.

2. Q: How is the weather now?
   A: It <u>is sunny and hot</u>.

   Q: 지금 날씨가 어떤가요?
   A: 화창하고 더워요.

3. Q: How does he look?
   A: He <u>looks healthy</u>.

   Q: 그는 어때 보이나요?
   A: 그는 건강해 보여요.

pp.28-29

A

Q a: What color is the umbrella?
그 우산은 무슨 색인가요?

모범 답안 The umbrella is yellow.
그 우산은 노란색이에요.

필수 어휘
what color 무슨 색 / umbrella 우산 / yellow 노랑

해설
그림 속 우산의 색깔이 무엇인지를 대답해야 하므로 우선 그림 속 우산이 무슨 색인지를 파악해야 합니다. 우산은 노란색이므로 'The umbrella / is yellow.' 라고 말하세요.

Q b: Is the food delicious?
그 음식은 맛있나요?

모범 답안 Yes, it is delicious.
네, 맛있어요.

필수 어휘
food 음식 / delicious 맛있는

해설
음식이 맛있는지를 묻는 be동사 Yes / No 질문입니다. 그림에서 소년의 눈이 커지고, 웃으며 수저질을 하는 것은 '음식이 맛있다'는 의미이므로 'Yes, it is delicious.' 라고 말하세요.

Q c: Is the book interesting?
그 책은 재미있나요?

모범 답안 No, it isn't. It is boring.
아니요. 그것은 지루해요.

필수 어휘
book 책 / interesting 재미있는 / boring 지루한, 재미없는

해설
소녀가 책을 편 채 쿨쿨 자고 있으므로 책이 재미있지 않고 지루하다는 뜻입니다. 그러므로 책이 재미있는지 아닌지에 대한 be동사 Yes / No 질문에는 '아니요, 그렇지 않아요. 그 책은 지루해요.' 즉, 'No, it isn't. It is boring.' 이라고 말하세요.

B

Q a: How is the test?
그 시험은 어때요?

모범 답안 The test is difficult.
그 시험은 어려워요.

필수 어휘
how 어떻게, 어떤 / test 시험 / difficult 어려운

해설
소년이 머리를 긁적이며 난감해하는 표정을 짓고 있으므로 '시험은 어떤가요?' 라는 질문에 '시험이 어려워요.' 라고 말해야 하므로 'The test / is difficult.' 라고 말하세요.

Q b: How is the weather?
날씨가 어떤가요?

모범 답안 The weather is windy.
바람이 많이 불어요.

필수 어휘
How is the weather? 날씨가 어떤가요? / weather 날씨 / windy 바람 부는

해설
여자의 머리와 옷이 바람에 날리는 것으로 보아 바람이 부는 날씨입니다. 그러므로 'The weather / is windy.' 라고 말하세요.

Q c: Is the girl happy?
그 소녀는 행복한가요?

모범 답안 No, she isn't. She is sad.
아니요. 그녀는 슬퍼요.

필수 어휘
happy 즐거운 / sad 슬픈

해설
소녀가 행복한지를 묻는 be동사 Yes / No 질문입니다. 소녀가 40이라고 적혀 있는 종이를 보고 울 듯한 표정을 짓고 있으므로 우선 '아니요, 그렇지 않아요.' 라는 'No, she isn't.' 을 말하고 이어서 '그녀는 슬퍼요.' 라는 'She is sad.' 를 말하세요.

Unit 03 그림 속 장소 / 위치 설명하기

표현 연습 p.31

A 1. in front of 2. in
3. on 4. next to

A

1. The cars are <u>in front of</u> the building.
   차들이 건물 앞에 있다.

2. The girl is studying <u>in</u> the library.
   그 소녀는 도서관에서 공부하고 있다.

3. They are walking <u>on</u> the bridge.
   그들은 다리 위를 걷고 있다.

4. The woman is standing <u>next to</u> the bus stop.
   여자가 버스 정류장 옆에 서 있다.

기본 말하기 p.32

A 1. on, under 2. in, next to
3. in front of, in 4. under, on

A

1. The laptop computer is <u>on</u> the table.
   The laptop computer is not <u>under</u> the table.

   그 노트북 컴퓨터는 테이블 위에 있다.
   그 노트북 컴퓨터는 테이블 아래에 있지 않다.

2. They are playing <u>in</u> the water.
   They are not playing <u>next to</u> the water.

   그들은 물속에서 놀고 있다.
   그들은 물 옆에서 놀고 있지 않다.

3. The man is <u>in front of</u> the building.
   The man is not <u>in</u> the building.

   그 남자는 그 건물 앞에 있다.
   그 남자는 그 건물 안에 있지 않다.

4. They are sitting <u>under</u> the parasol.
   They are not sitting <u>on</u> the parasol.

   그들은 파라솔 아래에 앉아 있다.
   그들은 파라솔 위에 앉아 있지 않다.

심화 말하기 p.33

A 1. at 2. on 3. in 4. next to

A

1. A boy is buying flowers <u>at</u> the flower shop.
   한 소년이 꽃가게에서 꽃을 사고 있다.

2. A man is sitting <u>on</u> the chair.
   한 남자가 의자 위에 앉아 있다.

3. A woman is eating <u>in</u> the restaurant.
   한 여자가 식당 안에서 식사를 하고 있다.

4. A man is standing <u>next to</u> the car.
   한 남자가 차 옆에 서 있다.

실전 유형 대비하기 pp.34-35

A 1. in the office
2. on the playground
3. at the bus stop

C 1. next to the bookstore
2. at the supermarket
3. in front of the police station

A

1. Q: Is the man working in the office?
   A: Yes, he is working <u>in the office</u>.

   Q: 그 남자는 사무실에서 일하고 있나요?
   A: 네, 그는 사무실에서 일하고 있어요.

2. Q: Are the children reading books in the
   bookstore?

A: No, they aren't. They are playing <u>on the playground</u>.

Q: 그 아이들은 서점에서 책을 읽고 있나요?

A: 아니요. 그들은 놀이터에서 놀고 있어요.

3. Q: Is the girl eating in the restaurant?

A: No, she isn't. She is waiting for the bus <u>at the bus stop</u>.

Q: 그 소녀는 식당에서 식사를 하고 있나요?

A: 아니요. 그녀는 버스 정류장에서 버스를 기다리고 있어요.

C

1. Q: Where are the trees?

A: They are <u>next to the bookstore</u>.

Q: 그 나무들은 어디 있나요?

A: 그것들은 서점 옆에 있어요.

2. Q: Where are they now?

A: They are <u>at the supermarket</u>.

Q: 그들은 지금 어디 있나요?

A: 그들은 슈퍼마켓에 있어요.

3. Q: Where is the man standing?

A: He is standing <u>in front of the police station</u>.

Q: 그 남자는 어디에 서 있나요?

A: 그는 경찰서 앞에 서 있어요.

단원 평가

pp.36-37

A

Q a: Where are they now?
그들은 어디에 있나요?

[모범 답안] They are on / at / in the mountain.
그들은 산에 있어요.

[필수 어휘]
where 어디 / now 지금 / on ~위에 / at ~에 / in ~안 /
mountain 산

[해설]
그들이 어디에 있는지를 묻고 있으므로 그림 속 주인공들이 있는 장소를 살펴 봅니다. 산등성이, 나무, 흙길이 있는 것으로 보아 그들은 산에 있습니다. 이 때 '산 속에, 산에, 산 위에'라고 모두 표현 할 수 있습니다. 그러므로 'They are / on the mountain.' 또는 'They are / at the mountain.' 또는 'They are / in the mountain.'이라고 말하세요.

Q b: Are they playing in the park?
그들은 공원에서 놀고 있나요?

[모범 답안] No, they are not playing in the park. They are playing in the playground.
아니요, 그들은 공원에 있지 않아요. 그들은 놀이터에 있어요.

[필수 어휘]
playing 놀고 있는 / in the park 공원에서 /
in the playground 놀이터에서

[해설]
그들은 공원에서 놀고 있는지를 묻는 be동사 Yes / No 질문입니다. 아이들이 놀고 있는 장소는 공원이 아니라 놀이터이므로 우선 '아니요, 그들은 공원에서 놀고 있지 않아요.'라는 'No, they aren't playing / in the park.라고 말한 뒤, '그들은 놀이터에서 놀고 있어요.'라는 'They are playing / in the playground.'라고 말하세요.

Q c: Where is the bus stop?
버스 정류장은 어디에 있나요?

[모범 답안] The bus stop is in front of the bookstore.
버스 정류장은 서점 앞에 있어요.

[필수 어휘]
where 어디 / bus stop 버스 정류장 / in front of ~ 앞에 /
bookstore 서점

[해설]
버스 정류장이 어디에 있는지를 묻고 있으므로 그림 속 버스 정류장과 주변 건물들을 살펴 봅니다. 버스 정류장을 가리키는 팻말이 'bookstore' 즉, 서점 앞에 있으므로 'The bookstore is / in front of the book store.'라고 말하세요.

B

Q a: Where is the girl studying?
그 소녀는 어디서 공부하고 있나요?

모범 답안 She is studying at / in the library.
그녀는 도서관에서 공부하고 있어요.

필수 어휘

where 어디 / studying 공부하고 있는 / at ~에서 /
in ~안에 / library 도서관

해설

소녀가 어디에서 공부하고 있는지를 묻고 있으므로 그림 속 소
녀가 어디에 있는 지를 살펴 봅니다. 책 선반에 많은 책이 있고
탁자 형태의 책상을 보아 이 곳이 도서관임을 알 수 있습니다.
그러므로 'She / is studying / at the library.' 또는 'She /
is studying / in the library.' 라고 말하세요.

Q b: Where is the cat?
그 고양이는 어디 있나요?

모범 답안 The cat is under the bench.
그 고양이는 벤치 아래에 있어요.

필수 어휘

where 어디 / cat 고양이 / under ~ 아래에 / bench 긴 의자

해설

고양이가 어디 있는지를 묻고 있으므로 그림 속 고양이가 어디
에 있는지를 살펴 봅니다. 고양이는 긴 의자 아래에 있으므로
'The cat is / under the bench.' 라고 말하세요.

Q c: Are they in the classroom?
그들은 교실에 있나요?

모범 답안 Yes, they are in the classroom.
네, 그들은 교실에 있어요.

필수 어휘

in the classroom 교실 안에

해설

그들은 교실 안에 있는지를 묻는 be동사 Yes / No 질문입니
다. 소년과 소녀가 칠판, 책상 등이 교실 안에 있으므로 '네, 그
들은 교실 안에 있어요.'라는 'Yes, / they are / in the
classroom.' 라고 답하세요.

Part 2 연계 질문에 답하기

Unit 04 학교 생활

표현 연습 p.43

A 1. study   **2.** take a violin lesson
    3. take an exam   **4.** have lunch

A

1. I study in the library.
나는 도서관에서 공부한다.

2. I take a violin lesson.
나는 바이올린 수업을 받는다.

3. I take an exam.
나는 시험을 친다.

4. I have lunch with my friends.
나는 내 친구들과 점심을 먹는다.

기본 말하기 p.44

A 1. at 8:30, at about 8 o'clock
    2. five classes, seven classes
    3. very nice, friendly
    4. study in the library, take a piano lesson

A

1. Q: What time do you go to school?
A: I go to school at 8:30.
I go to school at about 8 o'clock.

Q: 너는 몇 시에 학교에 가니?
A: 나는 8시 30분에 학교에 가.
나는 8시경에 학교에 가.

2. Q: How many classes do you have a day?
   A: I have <u>five classes</u> a day.
      I have <u>seven classes</u> a day.

   Q: 하루에 수업이 몇 시간이니?
   A: 하루에 수업이 5시간 있어.
      하루에 수업이 7시간 있어.

3. Q: How are your classmates?
   A: They're <u>very nice</u>.
      They're <u>friendly</u>.

   Q: 너의 반 친구들은 어떠니?
   A: 그들은 아주 좋아.
      그들은 다정해.

4. Q: What do you do after class?
   A: I <u>study in the library</u>.
      I <u>take a piano lesson</u>.

   Q: 너는 방과 후에 무엇을 하니?
   A: 나는 도서관에서 공부를 해.
      나는 피아노 수업을 들어.

심화 말하기 p.45

A 1. English, math
   2. Mr. Johnson, Ms. Jung
   3. great, kind
   4. at 3 p.m., at 5 in the afternoon

A

1. Q: What is your next class?
   A: It's <u>English</u>.
      It's <u>math</u>.

   Q: 네 다음 수업은 뭐니?
   A: 영어야.
      수학이야.

2. Q: Who teaches the class?
   A: <u>Mr. Johnson</u> teaches the class.
      <u>Ms. Jung</u> teaches the class.

   Q: 누가 그 수업을 가르치시지?
   A: 존슨(Johnson) 선생님이 그 수업을 가르치셔.
      정 선생님이 그 수업을 가르치셔.

3. Q: How is he / she?
   A: He / She is <u>great</u>.
      He / She is <u>kind</u>.

   Q: 그분은 어떤 분이시니?
   A: 그분은 아주 좋으셔.
      그분은 친절하셔.

4. Q: When do you finish the class?
   A: I finish the class <u>at 3 p.m.</u>
      I finish the class <u>at 5 in the afternoon</u>.

   Q: 그 수업은 언제 끝나니?
   A: 오후 3시에 수업이 끝나.
      오후 5시에 수업이 끝나.

실전 유형 대비하기 pp.46-47

A 1. from 12:30 to 1:30
   2. in the school cafeteria
   3. PE and art class
   4. play soccer

C 1. is English   2. is interesting
   3. Kate teaches   4. is helpful

A

1. Q a: When is lunch time?
   점심시간이 언제지?

   Your answer: It is <u>from 12:30 to 1:30</u>.
   12시 30분부터 1시 30분까지야.

2. Q b: Where do you have lunch?
   너는 어디서 점심을 먹니?

   Your answer: I have lunch <u>in the school cafeteria</u>.
   나는 학교 식당에서 점심을 먹어.

3. Q c: What classes do you have in the afternoon?
   너는 오후에 무슨 수업이 있니?

   Your answer: I have PE and art class.
   체육과 미술 수업이 있어.

4. Q d: What will you do after class?
   너는 방과 후에 뭘 할 거니?

   Your answer: I will play soccer with friends.
   친구들과 축구를 할 거야.

C

1. Q a: What is your favorite subject?
   네가 가장 좋아하는 과목은 무엇이니?

   Your answer: My favorite subject is English.
   내가 가장 좋아하는 과목은 영어야.

2. Q b: Why do you like it?
   왜 그것을 좋아하니?

   Your answer: It is interesting.
   그것은 재미있어.

3. Q c: Who teaches it?
   누가 그것을 가르치시니?

   Your answer: Kate teaches it.
   케이트(Kate) 선생님이 그것을 가르치셔.

4. Q d: How is the teacher?
   그 선생님은 어떤 분이시니?

   Your answer: She is helpful.
   도움을 많이 주는 분이셔.

단원 평가

pp.48-49

A

Q a: When do you go to school?
   너는 언제 학교에 가니?

모범 답안 I go to school at 8 o'clock.
   나는 8시에 학교에 가.

필수 어휘

when 언제 / go to school 학교에 가다 / at ~에 /
o'clock (몇) 시

해설

학교에 언제 가는지를 묻는 질문이므로 'I / go to school /
at 8 o'clock.' 처럼 '언제'에 관한 내용을 넣어서 완전한 문장
으로 답하세요.

Q b: How do you get to school?
   너는 학교에 어떻게 가니?

모범 답안 I take the bus to school.
   나는 버스를 타고 학교에 가.

필수 어휘

how 어떻게 / get to school 학교에 도착하다 /
take the bus 버스를 타다

해설

학교에 어떻게 도착하는지 방법을 묻는 질문이므로 'I / take
the bus / to school.' 처럼 '어떻게'에 대한 내용을 넣어서
완전한 문장으로 답하세요.

Q c: How long does it take?
   시간이 얼마나 걸리니?

모범 답안 It takes about thirty minutes.
   약 30분이 걸려.

필수 어휘

how long 얼마나 오랫동안 / take 시간이 ~ 걸리다 /
about 대략 / thirty 삼십 / minutes (몇)분

해설

학교까지 가는데 시간이 얼마나 걸리는지를 묻는 질문입니다.
'시간이 ~ 걸리다'라고 말할 때 주어 it으로 시작합니다. '대략
30분이 걸려요.'는 'It / takes / about thirty minutes.' 라
고 합니다.

Q d: What time does your first class start?
   첫 수업은 몇 시에 시작하니?

모범 답안 It starts at 8:30 in the morning.
   아침 8시 30분에 시작해.

what time 몇 시 / first class 첫 수업 / start 시작하다 /
at (몇 시)에 / in the morning 아침에

해설

첫 수업이 몇 시에 시작하냐는 질문이므로 'It / starts / at
8:30 / in the morning.' 처럼 '몇 시에' 시작하는지 내용을
넣어서 완전한 문장으로 답하세요.

B

Q a: When does your class begin?
네 수업은 언제 시작하니?

모범 답안 My class begins at 9 a.m.
수업은 9시에 시작해.

필수 어휘

when 언제 / your 너의 / class 수업 / my 나의 /
begin 시작하다 / at (몇 시)에

해설

너의 수업은 언제 시작하냐는 질문이므로 'My class /
begins / at 9 a.m.' 처럼 '언제'에 대한 내용을 넣어서 완전
한 문장으로 답하세요.

Q b: How many classes do you have a day?
하루에 수업이 몇 시간이니?

모범 답안 I have 5 classes a day.
하루에 수업이 5시간이야.

필수 어휘

how many classes 얼마나 많은 수업들 / a day 하루에

해설

하루에 수업이 몇 개냐는 질문이므로 'I / have / 5 classes /
a day.' 처럼 '몇 개의 수업'에 대한 내용을 넣어서 완전한 문
장으로 답하세요.

Q c: What is your favorite subject?
네가 가장 좋아하는 과목은 무엇이니?

모범 답안 My favorite subject is history.
내가 가장 좋아하는 과목은 역사야.

필수 어휘

what 무엇 / your 너의 / favorite 가장 좋아하는 /
subject 과목

해설

네가 가장 좋아하는 과목이 뭐냐는 질문이므로 'My favorite
subject / is / history.' 처럼 자신이 좋아하는 과목에 대한 내
용을 넣어서 완전한 문장으로 답하세요.

Q d: Why do you like the subject?
너는 그 과목을 왜 좋아하니?

모범 답안 I like history because it is very interesting.
매우 흥미로워서 나는 역사를 좋아해.

필수 어휘

why 왜 / subject 과목 / history 역사 / because 왜냐면 /
interesting 흥미로운

해설

왜 그 과목을 좋아하는지를 묻는 질문이므로 'I / like /
history / because / it is / very interesting.' 처럼 좋아하
는 이유에 대한 내용을 넣어서 완전한 문장으로 답하세요.

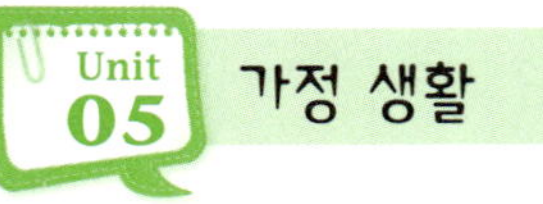

표현 연습   p.51

| A | 1. take a shower | 2. clean the room |
| | 3. wash the dishes | 4. take a walk |

A

1. I take a shower.
나는 샤워를 한다.

2. I clean the room.
나는 방을 청소한다.

3. I wash the dishes.
나는 설거지를 한다.

4. I take a walk with my dog.
   나는 강아지와 함께 산책을 한다.

기본 말하기 p.52

A

1. Q: What time do you get up?
   A: I get up at 7 o'clock.
      I get up at 7:40.

   Q: 너는 몇 시에 일어나니?
   A: 나는 7시에 일어나.
      나는 7시 40분에 일어나.

2. Q: What do you have for breakfast?
   A: I have cereal for breakfast.
      I have toast and juice for breakfast.

   Q: 너는 아침 식사로 무엇을 먹니?
   A: 나는 아침 식사로 시리얼을 먹어.
      나는 아침 식사로 토스트와 주스를 먹어.

3. Q: What do you do after dinner?
   A: I clean my room.
      I wash the dishes.

   Q: 저녁 식사 후에 무엇을 하니?
   A: 나는 내 방 청소를 해.
      나는 설거지를 해.

4. Q: When do you go to sleep?
   A: I go to sleep at 10 o'clock.
      I go to sleep after 10.

   Q: 너는 언제 자러 가니?
   A: 나는 10시에 자러 가.
      나는 10시 이후에 자러 가.

심화 말하기 p.53

A

1. Q: What time do you get up?
   A: I get up before 7.
      I get up at about 7:30.

   Q: 너는 몇 시에 일어나니?
   A: 나는 7시 전에 일어나.
      나는 약 7시 30분에 일어나.

2. Q: What do you do first in the morning?
   A: I brush my teeth.
      I wash my face.

   Q: 너는 아침에 제일 먼저 무엇을 하니?
   A: 나는 이를 닦아.
      나는 세수를 해.

3. Q: Who do you have breakfast with?
   A: I have breakfast with my family.
      I have breakfast with my sister.

   Q: 너는 누구와 아침을 먹니?
   A: 나는 가족과 아침을 먹어.
      나는 여동생과 아침을 먹어.

4. Q: When do you leave the house for school?
   A: I leave the house after breakfast.
      I leave the house at 8.

   Q: 너는 등교를 위해 언제 집을 나서니?
   A: 나는 아침 식사 후에 집을 나서.
      나는 8시에 집을 나서.

실전 유형 대비하기

A 1. at about 3 o'clock   2. take a shower
3. clean my room   4. take a walk

C 1. I like to watch TV.
2. I do my homework.
3. I wash the dishes
4. I go to bed around 10 o'clock.

A

1. Q a: When do you come back home from school?
너는 학교에서 언제 집으로 돌아오니?

Your answer: I come back home <u>at about 3 o'clock</u>.
나는 3시경에 집으로 돌아와.

2. Q b: What do you do when you come back home?
너는 집에 와서 무엇을 하니?

Your answer: I <u>take a shower</u> when I come back home.
나는 집에 와서 샤워를 해.

3. Q c: Do you also clean your room?
너는 네 방 청소도 하니?

Your answer: Yes, I <u>clean my room</u>.
응, 내 방 청소를 해.

4. Q d: What do you do after dinner?
너는 저녁 식사 후에 무엇을 하니?

Your answer: I <u>take a walk</u> after dinner.
나는 저녁 식사 후에 산책을 해.

C

1. Q a: What do you like to do at home?
너는 집에서 뭐 하는 걸 좋아하니?

Your answer: <u>I like to watch TV.</u>
나는 TV 보는 걸 좋아해.

2. Q b: What do you do before dinner?
너는 저녁 식사 전에 무엇을 하니?

Your answer: <u>I do my homework</u>.
나는 숙제를 해.

3. Q c: Do you help your mom?
너는 엄마를 도와드리니?

Your answer: Yes, I <u>wash the dishes</u> after dinner.
응, 나는 저녁 식사 후에 설거지를 해.

4. Q d: When do you go to bed?
너는 언제 자러 가니?

Your answer: <u>I go to bed around 10 o'clock.</u>
나는 10시 즈음 자러 가.

단원 평가

A

Q a: What time do you wake up?
너는 몇 시에 일어나니?

모범 답안 I wake up at 7 o'clock.
나는 7시에 일어나.

필수 어휘

what time 몇 시 / wake up 잠에서 깨다 / at (몇 시)에 / o'clock (몇) 시

해설

몇 시에 일어나냐는 질문이므로 'I / wake up / at 7 o'clock.' 처럼 '몇 시'에 해당하는 내용을 넣어서 완전한 문장으로 답하세요.

Q b: Do you have breakfast?
너는 아침을 먹니?

모범 답안 Yes, I always have breakfast.
응, 나는 항상 아침을 먹어.

필수 어휘

have breakfast 아침을 먹다 / always 항상

해설

아침 식사를 먹는지를 묻는 do동사 Yes / No 질문이므로 긍정 또는 부정의 표현을 넣어 'Yes, / I always / have breakfast.'처럼 완전한 문장으로 답하세요.

Q c: What do you do before you go to school?
　　학교 가기 전에 너는 무엇을 하니?

모범 답안　I pack my backpack.
　　　　　나는 내 책가방을 챙겨.

필수 어휘

what 무엇 / do 하다 / before ~ 하기 전에 /
go to school 학교에 가다 / pack 짐을 싸다 /
backpack 배낭 가방

해설

학교에 가기 전에 무엇을 하냐는 질문이므로 'I / pack / my backpack.'처럼 '무엇을 하다'에 해당하는 내용을 넣어서 완전한 문장으로 답하세요.

Q d: When do you leave your home?
　　너는 언제 집을 나서니?

모범 답안　I leave my home at 8 o'clock.
　　　　　나는 8시에 집을 나서.

필수 어휘

when 언제 / leave 떠나다 / home 집 / at (몇 시)에 /
o'clock (몇) 시

해설

언제 집을 나서냐는 질문이므로 'I / leave / my home / at 8 o'clock.'처럼 '언제'에 해당하는 내용을 넣어서 완전한 문장으로 답하세요.

B

Q a: What time do you come back home?
　　너는 언제 집으로 돌아오니?

모범 답안　I come back home after 4 p.m.
　　　　　나는 오후 4시 이후에 집으로 돌아와.

필수 어휘

what time 몇 시 / come back 돌아오다 / home 집으로 /
after ~후에 / p.m. 오후

해설

몇 시에 집에 오냐는 질문이므로 'I / come back / home / after 4 p.m.'처럼 '몇 시'에 해당하는 내용을 넣어서 완전한 문장으로 답하세요.

Q b: What do you do after you come back home?
　　집에 와서 너는 무엇을 하니?

모범 답안　I take a shower.
　　　　　나는 샤워를 해.

필수 어휘

what 무엇 / after ~한 후에 /
come back home 집에 돌아오다 /
take a shower 샤워를 하다

해설

집에 돌아온 후 무엇을 하냐는 질문이므로 'I / take a shower.'처럼 '무엇을 하다'에 해당하는 내용을 넣어서 완전한 문장으로 답하세요.

Q c: What do you do after dinner?
　　너는 저녁 식사 후에는 무엇을 하니?

모범 답안　I do my homework and watch TV.
　　　　　나는 숙제를 하고 TV를 봐.

필수 어휘

what 무엇 / do 하다 / after dinner 저녁식사 후에 /
do my homework 내 숙제를 하다 / watch TV TV를 보다

해설

저녁 식사 후에 뭘 하냐는 질문이므로 'I / do my homework / and / watch TV.'처럼 '무엇을 하다'에 해당하는 내용을 넣어서 완전한 문장으로 답하세요.

Q d: When do you go to sleep?
　　너는 언제 자러 가니?

모범 답안　I go to sleep after 10 p.m.
　　　　　나는 밤 10시 이후에 자러 가.

필수 어휘

when 언제 / go to sleep 잠자리에 들다 / after ~후에 /
p.m. 오후

언제 자냐는 질문이므로 'I / go to sleep / after 10 p.m.' 처럼 '언제'에 해당하는 내용을 넣어서 완전한 문장으로 답하세요.

Unit 06 사회 활동

표현 연습 p.59

A 1. introduce   2. visit
    3. join   4. meet

A

1. I introduce myself.
   제 소개를 하겠습니다.

2. I visit my grandparents.
   나는 할아버지, 할머니를 방문한다.

3. I'd like to join a drama club.
   나는 연극 동아리에 가입하고 싶다.

4. We meet our friends at the library.
   우리는 도서관에서 친구들을 만난다.

기본 말하기 p.60

A 1. my friends, my classmates
    2. a library, a park
    3. read books, take a walk
    4. school life, our favorite singers

A

1. Q: Who do you meet outside?
   A: I meet my friends.
       I meet my classmates.

   Q: 너는 밖에서 누구를 만나니?
   A: 나는 내 친구들을 만나.
       나는 우리 반 친구들을 만나.

2. Q: Where do you go with them?
   A: I go to a library with them.
       I go to a park with them.

   Q: 너는 그들과 어디를 가니?
   A: 나는 그들과 함께 도서관에 가.
       나는 그들과 함께 공원에 가.

3. Q: What do you do with them?
   A: I read books with them.
       I take a walk with them.

   Q: 너는 그들과 무엇을 하니?
   A: 나는 그들과 책을 읽어.
       나는 그들과 산책을 해.

4. Q: What do you talk about with them?
   A: We talk about school life.
       We talk about our favorite singers.

   Q: 너는 그들과 무엇에 대해 이야기하니?
   A: 우리는 학교생활에 대해 이야기해.
       우리는 우리가 좋아하는 가수에 대해 이야기해.

심화 말하기 p.61

A 1. a soccer club, a dancing club
    2. play soccer, practice dancing
    3. on the playground, in the gym
    4. good for my health, make friends

A

1. Q: What club are you in?
   A: I am in a soccer club.
       I am in a dancing club.

   Q: 너는 무슨 동아리에 속해 있니?
   A: 나는 축구 동아리 소속이야.
       나는 댄싱 동아리 소속이야.

2. Q: What do you do in the club?
   A: I play soccer with my friends.
       I practice dancing with the club members.

Q: 너는 그 동아리에서 무엇을 하니?
A: 나는 친구들과 축구를 해.
   나는 동아리 회원들과 춤 연습을 해.

3. Q: Where does your club meet?
   A: We meet <u>on the playground</u>.
      We meet <u>in the gym</u>.

   Q: 네 동아리는 어디에서 만나니?
   A: 우리는 운동장에서 만나.
      우리는 체육관에서 만나.

4. Q: Why are you in the club?
   A: Because it is <u>good for my health</u>.
      Because I can <u>make friends</u>.

   Q: 너는 왜 그 동아리에 들어갔니?
   A: 왜냐면 건강에 좋으니까.
      왜냐면 친구들을 사귈 수 있으니까.

실전 유형 대비하기 pp.62-63

A 1. this Friday
2. ten friends
3. at home
4. pretty clothes

C 1. I help old people
2. I do it once a week.
3. I do it with my classmates.
4. I feel great.

A

1. Q a: When will you have your birthday party?
      너는 언제 네 생일 파티를 열 거니?

   Your answer: I will have my birthday party <u>this Friday</u>.
      나는 이번 주 금요일에 내 생일 파티를 열 거야.

2. Q b: How many friends will you invite to your party?
      너는 파티에 친구 몇 명을 초대할 거니?

   Your answer: I will invite <u>ten friends</u>.
      나는 친구 열 명을 초대할 거야.

3. Q c: Where will you have your birthday party?
      너는 어디에서 생일 파티를 열 거니?

   Your answer: I will have my birthday party <u>at home</u>.
      나는 집에서 생일 파티를 열 거야.

4. Q d: What gift do you want to get?
      너는 무슨 선물을 받고 싶니?

   Your answer: I want to get <u>pretty clothes</u>.
      나는 예쁜 옷을 받고 싶어.

C

1. Q a: Do you do any volunteer work?
      너는 자원 봉사 활동을 하니?

   Your answer: Yes, <u>I help old people</u>.
      응, 나는 어르신들을 도와드려.

2. Q b: How often do you do it?
      너는 얼마나 자주 그 일을 하니?

   Your answer: <u>I do it once a week</u>.
      나는 일주일에 한 번 그 일을 해.

3. Q c: Who do you do it with?
      너는 누구와 그 일을 하니?

   Your answer: <u>I do it with my classmates</u>.
      나는 우리 반 친구들과 그 일을 해.

4. Q d: How do you feel after the volunteer work?
      너는 그 봉사 활동 후에 기분이 어떠니?

   Your answer: <u>I feel great</u>.
      기분이 매우 좋아.

A

Q a: What kind of food would you like to eat?
너는 어떤 종류의 음식을 먹고 싶니?

모범 답안 I'd like to eat hamburgers.
나는 햄버거를 먹고 싶어.

필수 어휘

what kind of food 어떤 종류의 음식 /
would you like to ~? ~을 하고 싶니? / eat 먹다 /
I'd like to ~. ~을 하고 싶다. / hamburgers 햄버거

해설

어떤 종류의 음식을 먹고 싶냐는 질문이므로 'I'd like to eat /
hamburgers.' 처럼 '무엇'에 해당하는 내용을 넣어서 완전한
문장으로 답하세요.

Q b: What kind of restaurant would you like to go to?
너는 어떤 종류의 식당에 가고 싶니?

모범 답안 I would like to go to King's Burger.
나는 킹즈 버거(King's Burger)에 가고 싶어.

필수 어휘

what kind of restaurant 어떤 종류의 식당 /
would you like to ~? ~을 하고 싶니? / go to ~로 가다

해설

어떤 종류의 식당에 가고 싶냐는 질문이므로 'I would like to
go / to King's Burger.' 처럼 '어떤 식당'에 해당하는 내용을
넣어서 완전한 문장으로 답하세요.

Q c: Where is the restaurant?
그 식당은 어디에 있니?

모범 답안 It is next to the supermarket.
그 식당은 슈퍼마켓 옆에 있어.

필수 어휘

where 어디 / restaurant 식당 / next to ~옆에 /
supermarket 슈퍼마켓

해설

그 식당이 어디에 있냐는 질문이므로 'It is / next to the
supermarket.' 처럼 위치를 설명하는 내용을 넣어서 완전한
문장으로 답하세요.

Q d: How far is the restaurant from here?
여기서 그 식당까지 거리가 얼마나 머니?

모범 답안 It is close from here.
그 식당은 여기서 가까워.

필수 어휘

how far 얼마나 먼 / restaurant 식당 /
from here 여기에서 / close 가까운

해설

그 식당이 여기서 얼마나 머냐는 질문이므로 'It is close /
from here.' 처럼 '얼마나 먼지' 또는 '가깝다' 등의 내용을 넣
어서 완전한 문장으로 답하세요.

B

Q a: Do you meet your friends outside?
너는 밖에서 친구들을 만나니?

모범 답안 Yes, I meet my friends outside.
응, 밖에서 친구들을 만나.

필수 어휘

meet 만나다 / your friends 너의 친구들 / outside 밖에서

해설

친구들과 밖에서 만나냐는 do동사 Yes / No 질문이므로 일단
'네, 그래요.' 또는 '아니요, 그렇지 않아요.' 라는 긍정 또는 부
정을 말해야 합니다. 그런 후 'Yes, / I / meet / my friends /
outside.' 처럼 완전한 문장으로 답하세요.

Q b: How often do you meet them?
얼마나 자주 그들을 만나니?

모범 답안 I meet them every day.
나는 매일 그들을 만나.

필수 어휘

how often 얼마나 자주 / meet 만나다 / them 그들을 /
every day 매일

해설

얼마나 자주 친구들을 만나냐는 질문이므로 'I / meet / them /
every day.' 처럼 '얼마나 자주'에 해당하는 내용을 넣어서 완
전한 문장으로 답하세요.

Q c: Where do you go with them?

너는 그들과 어디를 가니?

 We usually go to a fast food restaurant.

우리는 주로 패스트푸드점에 가.

where 어디 / with them 그들과 함께 / usually 주로 /
fast food restaurant 패스트 푸드점

친구들과 함께 어디에 가냐는 질문이므로 'We / usually / go /
to a fast food restaurant.' 처럼 '어디'에 해당하는 내용을
넣어서 완전한 문장으로 답하세요.

Q d: What do you usually do with them?

너는 그들과 주로 무엇을 하니?

 We talk about our school life.

우리는 우리 학교 생활에 대해 이야기해.

what 무엇 / usually 주로 / do 하다 /
with them 그들과 함께 / talk about ~에 대해 얘기하다 /
our 우리의 / school life 학교 생활

친구들과 주로 무엇을 하냐는 질문이므로 'We / talk / about
our school life.' 처럼 '무엇을 하는지'에 대한 내용을 넣어서
완전한 문장으로 답하세요.

여가 생활

표현 연습

p.67

A 1. am interested in   2. draw a picture
   3. take a trip   4. ride a bicycle

A

1. I am interested in baseball.

   나는 야구에 관심이 있다.

2. I draw a picture in my free time.

   나는 여가 시간에 그림을 그린다.

3. I will take a trip to the beach this weekend.

   나는 이번 주말에 바닷가로 여행갈 것이다.

4. I ride a bicycle for exercise.

   나는 운동으로 자전거를 탄다.

기본 말하기

p.68

A 1. Japan, France   2. shopping, French food
   3. Asia, Europe   4. by plane, by ship

A

1. Q: What country would you like to go to?
   A: I'd like to go to Japan.
      I'd like to go to France.

   Q: 너는 어떤 나라에 가보고 싶니?
   A: 나는 일본에 가보고 싶어.
      나는 프랑스에 가보고 싶어.

2. Q: Why do you want to go there?
   A: I like shopping.
      I like French food.

   Q: 너는 왜 거기에 가고 싶니?
   A: 나는 쇼핑을 좋아하거든.
      나는 프랑스 음식을 좋아하거든.

3. Q: Where is the country?
   A: It is in Asia.
      It is in Europe.

   Q: 그 나라는 어디에 있니?
   A: 아시아에 있어.
      유럽에 있어.

4. Q: How can you travel to the country?
   A: I can travel by plane.
      I can travel by ship.

Q: 어떻게 그 나라로 여행갈 수 있니?

A: 비행기로 여행할 수 있어.

　　배로 여행할 수 있어.

심화 말하기　　　　　　　　　　　　p.69

> **A** 1. summer, winter
> 2. rain, snow
> 3. hot, cold
> 4. swimming, making a snowman

A

1. Q: What is your favorite season?

   A: My favorite season is <u>summer</u>.

   　　My favorite season is <u>winter</u>.

   Q: 네가 가장 좋아하는 계절은 뭐니?

   A: 내가 가장 좋아하는 계절은 여름이야.

   　　내가 가장 좋아하는 계절은 겨울이야.

2. Q: Why do you like the season?

   A: I like <u>rain</u>.

   　　I like <u>snow</u>.

   Q: 너는 그 계절을 왜 좋아하니?

   A: 나는 비를 좋아하거든.

   　　나는 눈을 좋아하거든.

3. Q: What kind of weather do you like?

   A: I like <u>hot</u> weather.

   　　I like <u>cold</u> weather.

   Q: 너는 어떤 날씨를 좋아하니?

   A: 나는 더운 날씨를 좋아해.

   　　나는 추운 날씨를 좋아해.

4. Q: What do you do during the season?

   A: I enjoy <u>swimming</u>.

   　　I enjoy <u>making a snowman</u>.

   Q: 그 계절에 너는 무엇을 하니?

   A: 나는 수영을 즐겨.

   　　나는 눈사람 만드는 것을 즐겨.

실전 유형 대비하기　　　　　　　　pp.70-71

> **A** 1. the zoo.
> 2. many kinds of animals.
> 3. Dolphins
> 4. by subway.

> **C** 1. Baseball and soccer are popular.
> 2. I like basketball the most.
> 3. I play it with my friends.
> 4. I play it every Sunday.

A

1. Q a: What place would you like to visit?
   너는 어떤 곳을 가보고 싶니?

   Your answer: I would like to visit <u>the zoo</u>.
   나는 동물원에 가고 싶어.

2. Q b: What can you see there?
   거기에서 뭘 볼 수 있는데?

   Your answer: I can see <u>many kinds of animals</u>.
   여러 종류의 동물들을 볼 수 있어.

3. Q c: What is the most popular animal there?
   거기에서 가장 인기 있는 동물은 무엇이니?

   Your answer: <u>Dolphins</u> are the most popular.
   돌고래가 가장 인기 있어.

4. Q d: How can you go there?
   너는 어떻게 거기에 갈 수 있니?

   Your answer: I can go there <u>by subway</u>.
   지하철을 타고 거기에 갈 수 있어.

C

1. Q a: What kinds of sports are popular in Korea?
   한국에서는 어떤 종류의 스포츠가 인기가 있니?

   Your answer: <u>Baseball and soccer are popular</u>.
   야구와 축구가 인기 있어.

2. Q b: Which sport do you like the most?
어떤 스포츠를 너는 가장 좋아하니?

Your answer: I like basketball the most.
나는 농구를 가장 좋아해.

3. Q c: Who do you play it with?
너는 누구와 그것을 함께 하니?

Your answer: I play it with my friends.
나는 내 친구들과 함께 해.

4. Q d: How often do you play it?
너는 얼마나 자주 그것을 하니?

Your answer: I play it every Sunday.
나는 일요일마다 그것을 해.

단원 평가

pp.72-73

A

Q a: What kinds of books do you like the most?
너는 어떤 종류의 책을 가장 좋아하니?

모범 답안 I like to read stories the most.
나는 이야기 책 읽는 것을 가장 좋아해.

필수 어휘

what kinds of books 어떤 종류의 책들을 /
the most 가장 많이 / stories 스토리, 이야기

해설

어떤 종류의 책들을 가장 좋아하냐는 질문이므로 'I / like to read / stories / the most.' 처럼 '어떤 종류의 책'에 대한 내용을 넣어서 완전한 문장으로 답하세요.

Q b: When do you read?
너는 언제 책을 읽니?

모범 답안 I read before bedtime.
나는 잠자기 전에 책을 읽어.

필수 어휘

when 언제 / read 책을 읽다 / before bedtime 자기 전

해설

언제 책을 읽냐는 질문이므로 'I / read / before bedtime.' 처럼 '언제'에 대한 내용을 넣어서 완전한 문장으로 답하세요.

Q c: Where do you usually read?
너는 주로 어디서 책을 읽니?

모범 답안 I read at home.
나는 집에서 책을 읽어.

필수 어휘

where 어디 / usually 주로 / read 책을 읽다 /
at home 집에서

해설

주로 어디에서 책을 읽냐는 질문이므로 'I / read / at home.' 처럼 '어디'에 대한 내용을 넣어서 완전한 문장으로 답하세요.

Q d: How many books do you read a month?
너는 한 달에 얼마나 많은 책을 읽니?

모범 답안 I read one book a month.
나는 한 달에 한 권의 책을 읽어.

필수 어휘

how many books 얼마나 많은 책들을 / a month 한 달에

해설

한 달에 얼마나 많은 책을 읽냐는 질문이므로 'I / read / one book / a month.' 처럼 '몇 권'에 대한 내용을 넣어서 완전한 문장으로 답하세요.

B

Q a: What is your favorite food?
네가 가장 좋아하는 음식은 무엇이니?

모범 답안 My favorite food is pizza.
내가 가장 좋아하는 음식은 피자야.

필수 어휘

what 무엇 / favorite 가장 좋아하는 / food 음식 / pizza 피자

해설

가장 좋아하는 음식이 뭐냐는 질문이므로 'My favorite food / is pizza.' 처럼 '가장 좋아하는 음식'에 대한 내용을 넣어서 완전한 문장으로 답하세요.

Q b: Where do you eat it?

너는 그것을 어디서 먹니?

모범 답안 I eat pizza at a Pizzaria.

나는 Pizzaria에서 피자를 먹어.

필수 어휘

where 어디 / eat 먹다 / at ~에서

해설

그것을 어디에서 먹냐는 질문이므로 'I / eat / pizza / at a Pizzaria.' 처럼 '어디'에 해당하는 내용을 넣어서 완전한 문장으로 답하세요.

Q c: Why do you like it?

너는 그것을 왜 좋아하니?

모범 답안 Because it is delicious.

왜냐하면 맛있으니까.

필수 어휘

why 왜 / like 좋아하다 / because 왜냐면 / delicious 맛있는

해설

왜 그 음식을 좋아하냐는 질문이므로 'I / like / it / because / it is delicious.' 처럼 '좋아하는 이유'에 해당하는 내용을 넣어서 완전한 문장으로 답하세요.

Q d: How often do you eat it?

너는 얼마나 자주 그것을 먹니?

모범 답안 I eat it once a week.

나는 일주일에 한 번 그것을 먹어.

필수 어휘

how often 얼마나 자주 / eat 먹다 / once 한 번 /
a week 일주일에

해설

얼마나 자주 그 음식을 먹냐는 질문이므로 'I / eat / it / once / a week.' 처럼 '얼마나 자주'에 해당하는 내용을 넣어서 완전한 문장으로 답하세요.

Part 3 그림 묘사하기

Unit 08 야외 활동

표현 연습   p.79

A 1. runs   2. goes shopping
    3. plays   4. takes a picture

A

1. A woman runs in the park.
한 여자가 공원에서 달리기를 한다.

2. A girl goes shopping.
한 소녀가 쇼핑을 한다.

3. A boy plays with a ball.
한 소년이 공을 가지고 논다.

4. A man takes a picture.
한 남자가 사진을 찍는다.

기본 말하기   p.80

A 1. makes a snowman   2. takes a picture
    3. flies a kite   4. waters the plants

A

1. A boy makes a snowman.
한 소년이 눈사람을 만든다.

2. A girl takes a picture.
한 소녀가 사진을 찍는다.

3. A boy flies a kite.
한 소년이 연을 날린다.

4. A girl waters the plants.
한 소녀가 식물에 물을 준다.

A 1. He runs with his dog on the grass.
　2. A boy plays badminton with his friend.
　3. A boy plays basketball on the court.
　4. She rows a boat in the lake.

A

1. He runs with his dog on the grass.
그는 그의 개와 함께 잔디 위를 달린다.

2. A boy plays badminton with his friend.
한 소년이 친구와 함께 배드민턴을 친다.

3. A boy plays basketball on the court.
한 소년이 농구 코트에서 농구를 한다.

4. She rows a boat in the lake.
그녀는 호수에서 배를 젓는다.

A 1. walks to the playground　**2.** put on
　3. stand　　　　　　　　　**4.** throws the ball
　5. jumps up　　　　　　　　**6.** walks towards

C 1. walks out of　　　　　　**2.** buy
　3. walk along　　　　　　　**4.** on the swing
　5. says good bye　　　　　　**6.** gets home

A

1. A boy <u>walks to the playground</u> with his friend.
한 소년이 친구와 함께 운동장으로 걸어간다.

2. The two boys <u>put on</u> their gloves.
그 두 소년은 야구 글로브를 낀다.

3. And then the two boys <u>stand</u>.
그런 다음, 그 두 소년은 서 있다.

4. The boy <u>throws the ball</u> to his friend.
그 소년이 친구에게 공을 던진다.

5. The boy's friend <u>jumps up</u> to catch the ball.
그 소년의 친구가 뛰어올라 그 공을 잡는다.

6. Then the boy's friend <u>walks towards</u> him.
그러고 나서 그 소년의 친구가 그를 향해 걸어온다.

C

1. A boy <u>walks out of</u> the school with a girl.
한 소년이 한 소녀와 함께 학교 밖으로 걸어 나온다.

2. And they <u>buy</u> hamburgers at a fast food restaurant.
그러고 그들은 패스트푸드점에서 햄버거를 산다.

3. And then they <u>walk along</u> the park and eat their hamburgers.
그런 다음 그들은 공원을 따라 걸으며 햄버거를 먹는다.

4. They play <u>on the swing</u>.
그들은 그네를 탄다.

5. Then the boy <u>says good bye</u> to the girl.
그러고 나서 그 소년이 그 소녀에게 작별인사를 한다.

6. Finally, the boy <u>gets home</u>.
마지막으로, 그 소년은 집에 도착한다.

A

모범 답안

The boy puts on clothes. And he packs up his bag. Then he leaves the house. He gets on the bus. Then he builds a tent with his friend. Finally he camps out with his friends.

소년이 옷을 입는다. 그리고 그는 자신의 가방을 싼다. 그리고 나서 그는 집을 나선다. 그는 버스를 탄다. 그런 뒤 그는 친구와 텐트를 친다. 마지막으로 그는 친구들과 야영을 한다.

필수 어휘

put on ~을 입다 / clothes 옷 / pack up 가방을 싸다 /
then 그리고 나서 / leave ~를 떠나나 /

get on the bus 버스를 타다 / build 세우다 / tent 텐트 /
with his friend 그의 친구와 함께 / finally 마침내 /
camp out 야영하다

6개의 그림을 보고 이야기를 구성하기 위해서는 모든 그림을
본 뒤 하나의 이어지는 이야기를 만들어야 합니다. 첫 번째 그
림의 중요 표현은 'put on clothes', 두 번째 그림의 중요 표
현은 'pack up his bag', 세 번째 그림의 중요 표현은
'leave the house', 네 번째 그림의 중요 표현은 'get on
the bus', 다섯 번째 그림의 중요 표현은 'build a tent', 여
섯 번째 그림의 중요 표현은 'camp out'입니다. 이 때 단순
현재 시제로 말하도록 하며, 주어가 3인칭 단수일 때 동사가
3인칭 변화하는 것을 잊지 말고 말하세요.

B

The boy puts on a soccer uniform. And he puts on
soccer shoes. He leaves the house with a ball. He
meets his friends on the playground. Then he plays
soccer with his friends. He drinks water with his
friends.

소년이 축구 유니폼을 입는다. 그리고 그는 축구화를 신는다.
그는 공을 갖고 집을 나선다. 그는 운동장에서 친구들을 만난
다. 그러고 나서 그는 친구들과 축구를 한다. 그는 친구들과 물
을 마신다.

puts on ~을 입다 / soccer uniform 축구 유니폼 /
soccer shoes 축구화 / leaves the house 집을 나서다 /
with a ball 공을 가지고 / meet 만나다 / playground 운동장 /
then 그리고 나서 / play soccer 축구를 하다 /
drink water 물을 마시다

6개의 그림을 보고 이야기를 구성하기 위해서는 모든 그림을
본 뒤 하나의 이어지는 이야기를 만들어야 합니다. 첫 번째 그
림의 중요 표현은 'put on a soccer uniform', 두 번째 그
림의 중요 표현은 'put on soccer shoes', 세 번째 그림의
중요 표현은 'leave the house with a ball', 네 번째 그림
의 중요 표현은 'meet his friends on the playground',
다섯 번째 그림의 중요 표현은 'play soccer', 여섯 번째 그

림의 중요 표현은 'drink water'입니다. 이 때 단순 현재 시
제로 말하도록 하며, 주어가 3인칭 단수일 때 동사가 3인칭 변
화하는 것을 잊지 말고 말하세요.

Unit 09 취미 / 오락 활동

표현 연습   p.87

A	1. watches	2. plays
	3. feeds	4. reads

A

1. A woman watches TV.
   한 여자가 TV를 본다.

2. A boy plays the guitar.
   한 소년이 기타를 친다.

3. A girl feeds the birds.
   한 소녀가 새에게 먹이를 준다.

4. A boy reads a book.
   한 소년이 책을 읽는다.

기본 말하기   p.88

A	1. sings a song	2. plays the flute
	3. listens to music	4. plays a computer game

A

1. A girl sings a song.
   한 소녀가 노래를 한다.

2. A girl plays the flute.
   한 소녀가 플루트를 분다.

3. A boy listens to music.
   한 소년이 음악을 듣는다.

4. A boy <u>plays a computer game</u>.
한 소년이 컴퓨터 게임을 한다.

> **A** 1. A boy feeds a dog.
> 2. He plays the violin.
> 3. A man plays tennis.
> 4. A boy plays darts on the wall.

A

1. A boy feeds a dog.
한 소년이 개에게 먹이를 준다.

2. He plays the violin.
그는 바이올린을 켠다.

3. A boy plays tennis with a girl.
한 남자가 테니스를 친다.

4. A boy plays darts on the wall.
한 소년이 벽에 걸린 다트 게임을 한다.

> **A** 1. walks on   2. sit on
> 3. use a laptop computer   4. stand up
> 5. passes a ball   6. walk out of
>
> **C** 1. amusement park   2. at the ticket booth
> 3. merry-go-round   4. ice cream
> 5. wait for   6. roller coaster

A

1. A boy <u>walks on</u> the grass with a girl.
한 소년이 한 소녀와 함께 잔디밭을 걷는다.

2. And they <u>sit on</u> the grass.
그리고 그들은 잔디밭 위에 앉는다.

3. Then they <u>use a laptop computer</u>.
그리고 나서 그들은 노트북 컴퓨터를 사용한다.

4. They <u>stand up</u> together.
그들은 함께 일어난다.

5. And then the boy <u>passes a ball</u> to the girl.
그런 다음 그 소년이 소녀에게 공을 패스한다.

6. Finally, they <u>walk out of</u> the grass.
마지막으로, 그들은 잔디밭을 걸어 나온다.

C

1. Two girls get to an <u>amusement park</u>.
두 소녀가 놀이공원에 도착한다.

2. They buy the tickets <u>at the ticket booth</u>.
그들은 매표소에서 표를 산다.

3. They ride a <u>merry-go-round</u>.
그들은 회전목마를 탄다.

4. They eat <u>ice cream</u>.
그들은 아이스크림을 먹는다.

5. They <u>wait for</u> the roller coaster.
그들은 롤러코스터를 기다린다.

6. Then they enjoy the <u>roller coaster</u>.
그러고 나서 그들은 롤러코스터를 타고 신나게 논다.

A

모범 답안

A boy goes on a trip with his family. And they arrive at the lake. He and his father fish by the lake. And his mother cooks near the tent. Then he has a meal with his family. Now he talks with his family.

한 소년이 가족과 여행을 간다. 그리고 그들은 호수에 도착한다. 그와 그의 아버지는 호숫가에서 낚시를 한다. 그리고 그의 어머니가 텐트 근처에서 요리를 한다. 그러고 나서 그는 가족과 함께 식사를 한다. 이제 그는 가족과 이야기를 나눈다.

go on a trip 여행을 가다 / with his family 그의 가족과 함께 /
arrive at ~에 도착하다 / lake 호수 / fish 낚시하다 /
by the lake 호숫가에서 / near ~가까이 / then 그리고 나서 /
have a meal 식사를 하다 / now 지금 /
talk with ~와 얘기하다

6개의 그림을 보고 이야기를 구성하기 위해서는 모든 그림을
본 뒤 하나의 이어지는 이야기를 만들어야 합니다. 첫 번째 그
림의 중요 표현은 'go on a trip with his family, 두 번째
그림의 중요 표현은 'arrive at the lake, 세 번째 그림의 중
요 표현은 'fish by the lake', 네 번째 그림의 중요 표현은
'his mother cooks', 다섯 번째 그림의 중요 표현은 'have
a meal', 여섯 번째 그림의 중요 표현은 'talk with his
family'입니다. 이때 단순 현재 시제로 말하도록 하며, 주어가
3인칭 단수일 때 동사가 3인칭 변화하는 것을 잊지 말고 말하
세요.

B

The girl calls someone. And then she meets her
friend. They put on helmets and take out the bikes.
Then they ride the bikes. And they drink water. Now
they sit on the bench and rest.

소녀가 누군가에게 전화를 건다. 그런 다음 그녀는 그녀의 친구
를 만난다. 그들은 헬멧을 쓰고 자전거를 꺼낸다. 그러고 나서
그들은 자전거를 탄다. 그리고 그들은 물을 마신다. 이제 그들
은 벤치에 앉아서 휴식을 취한다.

call someone 누군가에게 전화하다 / put on ~을 입다, 쓰다 /
helmet 헬멧 / take out ~을 꺼내다 / bike 자전거 /
ride the bikes 자전거를 타다 / rest 쉬다

6개의 그림을 보고 이야기를 구성하기 위해서는 모든 그림을
본 뒤 하나의 이어지는 이야기를 만들어야 합니다. 첫 번째 그
림의 중요 표현은 'call someone', 두 번째 그림의 중요 표
현은 'meet her friend', 세 번째 그림의 중요 표현은 'put
on helmets and take out the bikes', 네 번째 그림의 중
요 표현은 'ride the bikes', 다섯 번째 그림의 중요 표현은

'drink water', 여섯 번째 그림의 중요 표현은 'sit on the
bench and rest'입니다. 이 때 단순 현재 시제로 말하도록
하며, 주어가 3인칭 단수일 때 동사가 3인칭 변화하는 것을 잊
지 말고 말하세요.

Unit 10 개인 / 단체 활동

표현 연습 p.95

> **A 1.** sings in a chorus   **2.** writes in a diary
> **3.** watches a movie   **4.** works

A

1. He <u>sings in a chorus</u> with his classmates.
   그는 반 친구들과 함께 합창을 한다.

2. The girl <u>writes in a diary</u>.
   그 소녀가 일기를 쓴다.

3. A boy <u>watches a movie</u> with a friend.
   한 소년이 친구와 영화를 본다.

4. A boy <u>works</u> with his friend on the farm.
   한 소년이 농장에서 친구와 일을 한다.

기본 말하기 p.96

> **A 1.** gets up in the morning
> **2.** is in the museum
> **3.** works with dad
> **4.** has a meeting

A

1. A boy <u>gets up in the morning</u>.
   한 소년이 아침에 일어난다.

2. A girl <u>is in the museum</u>.
   한 소녀가 박물관에 있다.

3. A boy <u>works with dad</u>.
   한 소년이 아빠와 함께 일한다.

4. A woman <u>has a meeting</u>.
   한 여자가 회의를 한다.

심화 말하기   p.97

> **A** 1. He smiles at a girl.
>   2. She is in the meeting.
>   3. A boy eats a meal in the restaurant.
>   4. A girl gets a haircut.

A

1. He smiles at a girl.
   그는 한 소녀를 보고 미소 짓는다.

2. She is in the meeting.
   그녀는 회의 중이다.

3. A boy eats a meal in the restaurant.
   한 소년이 식당에서 밥을 먹는다.

4. A girl gets a haircut.
   한 소녀가 머리를 자른다.

실전 유형 대비하기   pp.98-99

> **A** 1. watches   2. gets up
>   3. walks to   4. reads
>   5. yawns   6. sleeps
>
> **C** 1. talk to   2. pick up
>   3. sweep the street 4. the poor girls
>   5. help   6. give presents

A

1. A boy <u>watches</u> TV on the sofa.
   한 소년이 소파에서 **TV**를 본다.

2. He <u>gets up</u> from the sofa.
   그는 소파에서 일어난다.

3. He <u>walks to</u> his room.
   그는 자기 방으로 걸어간다.

4. He <u>reads</u> a book at the desk.
   그는 책상에서 책을 읽는다.

5. He <u>yawns</u>.
   그는 하품을 한다.

6. Then he <u>sleeps</u> on the bed.
   그러고 나서 그는 침대에서 잠을 잔다.

C

1. Three girls <u>talk to</u> each other.
   세 명의 소녀들이 서로 이야기를 한다.

2. They <u>pick up</u> the trash.
   그들이 쓰레기를 줍는다.

3. They <u>sweep the street</u> near the house.
   그들이 집 근처의 거리를 빗자루로 쓴다.

4. Then they play with <u>the poor girls</u>.
   그러고 나서 그들은 불우한 소녀들과 함께 논다.

5. They <u>help</u> the poor girls eat lunch.
   그들은 그 불우한 소녀들이 점심 먹는 것을 도와준다.

6. They <u>give presents</u> to the poor girls.
   그들은 그 불우한 소녀들에게 선물을 준다.

단원 평가   pp.100-101

A

모범 답안

The three girls talk to each other. And then they eat ice cream. Now they see a movie in the theater. They eat popcorn. Then they have a meal together. Now they say 'goodbye' to each other.

세 소녀가 서로 이야기를 한다. 그런 다음 그들은 아이스크림을 먹는다. 이제 그들은 영화관에서 영화를 본다. 그들은 팝콘을 먹는다. 그러고 나서 그들은 함께 식사를 한다. 이제 그들은 서로에게 '잘 가' 하고 작별인사를 한다.

talk to ~에게 얘기하다 / each other 서로 / now 이제 /
see a movie 영화를 보다 / theater 극장 / popcorn 팝콘 /
have a meal 식사를 하다 / together 함께 /
say 'goodbye' 작별인사를 하다

6개의 그림을 보고 이야기를 구성하기 위해서는 모든 그림을 본 뒤 하나의 이어지는 이야기를 만들어야 합니다. 첫 번째 그림의 중요 표현은 'talk to each other', 두 번째 그림의 중요 표현은 'eat ice cream, 세 번째 그림의 중요 표현은 'see a movie', 네 번째 그림의 중요 표현은 'eat popcorn', 다섯 번째 그림의 중요 표현은 'have a meal together', 여섯 번째 그림의 중요 표현은 'say 'goodbye'' 입니다. 이 때 단순 현재 시제로 말하도록 하며, 주어가 3인칭 단수일 때 동사가 3인칭 변화하는 것을 잊지 말고 말하세요.

B

A boy meets his friends at the park. And the boy and his friends receive their waste bags. Then the boy and his friends go into the grass. And the boy and his friends pick up trash. The boy says "hello!" to other people. Finally the boy and his friends gather with their waste bags.

한 소년이 공원에서 친구들을 만난다. 그리고 그 소년과 그의 친구들이 쓰레기 봉투를 받는다. 그러고 나서 그 소년과 그의 친구들이 잔디밭으로 들어간다. 그리고 그 소년과 그의 친구들이 쓰레기를 줍는다. 그 소년이 다른 사람들에게 "안녕하세요" 하고 인사를 한다. 마지막으로 그 소년과 그의 친구들이 쓰레기 봉투를 들고 모인다.

meet 만나다 / at the park 공원에서 / receive 받다 /
waste bag 쓰레기 봉투 /
go into the grass 잔디밭으로 들어가다 / pick up 줍다 /
trash 쓰레기 / says "hello!" 인사를 하다 /
to other people 다른 사람들에게 / finally 마지막으로 /
gather 모으다

6개의 그림을 보고 이야기를 구성하기 위해서는 모든 그림을 본 뒤 하나의 이어지는 이야기를 만들어야 합니다. 첫 번째 그림의 중요 표현은 'meet his friends', 두 번째 그림의 중요 표현은 'receive their waste bags', 세 번째 그림의 중요 표현은 'go into the grass', 네 번째 그림의 중요 표현은 'pick up trash', 다섯 번째 그림의 중요 표현은 'say "hello!" to other people', 여섯 번째 그림의 중요 표현은 'gather with their waste bags' 입니다. 이 때 단순 현재 시제로 말하도록 하며, 주어가 3인칭 단수일 때 동사가 3인칭 변화하는 것을 잊지 말고 말하세요.

Part 4 문제 해결하기

Unit 11 거절하기

표현 연습
pp.106-107

A 1. I'm sorry, but I can't. / I am afraid I can't.
2. I am afraid I can't. / I'd love to, but I can't.
3. I'd love to, but I can't. / I'd like to, but I can't.

C 1. I am afraid
2. I am sorry / I'd love to / I'd like to
3. I am sorry / I'd love to / I'd like to
4. I am sorry / I'd love to / I'd like to

A

1. <u>I'm sorry, but I can't.</u> I am busy now.
미안하지만 안될 것 같아요. 나는 지금 바빠요.

   <u>I am afraid I can't.</u> I am busy now.
미안하지만 안될 것 같아요. 나는 지금 바빠요.

2. <u>I am afraid I can't.</u> I have to go home now.
미안하지만 안될 것 같아요. 나는 지금 집에 가야 해요.

   <u>I'd love to, but I can't.</u> I have to go home now.

나도 그러고 싶지만 안될 것 같아요. 나는 지금 집에 가야
해요.

3. I'd love to, but I can't. I don't have time now.
나도 그러고 싶지만 안될 것 같아요. 나는 지금 시간이 없
어요

I'd like to, but I can't. I don't have time now.
나고 그러고 싶지만 안될 것 같아요. 나는 지금 시간이 없
어요.

C

1. A: Would you like some coffee?
   B: I am afraid I can't. I don't like coffee.

   A: 커피 좀 드시겠어요?
   B: 미안하지만 안될 것 같아요. 저는 커피를 좋아하지 않
      아요.

2. A: Do you want to play a computer game with
      me?
   B: I am sorry, but I can't. I am busy now.
      I'd love to, but I can't. I am busy now.
      I'd like to, but I can't. I am busy now.

   A: 나랑 컴퓨터 게임 할래?
   B: 미안하지만 안될 것 같아. 지금 바빠.
      나도 그러고 싶지만 안될 것 같아. 지금 바빠.
      나도 그러고 싶지만 안될 것 같아. 지금 바빠.

3. A: How about playing badminton together?
   B: I am sorry, but I can't. I have to go back home.
      I'd love to, but I can't. I have to go back home.
      I'd like to, but I can't. I have to go back home.

   A: 같이 배드민턴 치는 거 어때?
   B: 미안하지만 안될 것 같아. 나 지금 집에 가야 돼.
      나도 그러고 싶지만 안될 것 같아. 나 지금 집에 가야 돼.
      나도 그러고 싶지만 안될 것 같아. 나 지금 집에 가야 돼.

4. A: Would you like to skate together?
   B: I am sorry, but I can't. I have a headache.
      I'd love to, but I can't. I have a headache.
      I'd like to, but I can't. I have a headache.

A: 같이 스케이트 탈래?
B: 미안하지만 안될 것 같아. 나 머리가 아파.
   나도 그러고 싶지만 안될 것 같아. 나 머리가 아파.
   나도 그러고 싶지만 안될 것 같아. 나 머리가 아파.

기본 말하기 p.108

A ① I'd love to, but I can't.
  ② I have to go home now.
  ③ I need to take care of my baby sister.
  ④ I am sorry.
  ⑤ But I can play soccer tomorrow.

A

① I'd love to, but I can't.
   나도 그러고 싶지만, 안될 것 같아.

② I have to go home now.
   나는 지금 집에 가야 해.

③ I need to take care of my baby sister.
   나는 아기 여동생을 돌봐야 해.

④ I am sorry.
   미안해.

⑤ But I can play soccer tomorrow.
   하지만 나 내일은 축구 할 수 있어.

심화 말하기 p.109

A ① sorry
  ② to play with you more, go home now
  ③ promised my mom, by 6 o'clock
  ④ So I need to

A

You're playing with your best friend. It's time to go
home. But your friend wants to play more with you.
You promised your mom you'd get back home by 6
o'clock. What would you say to your friend?

당신은 당신의 절친한 친구와 놀고 있습니다. 이제 집에 갈 시간입니다. 그러나 당신의 친구는 당신과 좀 더 놀고 싶어합니다. 당신은 엄마에게 6시까지 집에 가겠다고 약속을 했습니다. 당신은 친구에게 뭐라고 말하겠습니까?

① I'm sorry, but I can't.
미안하지만 안될 것 같아.

② I want to play with you more, but I have to go home now.
너와 더 놀고 싶지만 나는 지금 집에 가야 해.

③ I promised my mom I'd get back home by 6 o'clock.
엄마에게 6시까지 집에 가겠다고 약속했어.

④ So I need to get back home now. I'm sorry.
그래서 나 지금 집에 가야 돼. 미안해.

실전 유형 대비하기   pp.110-111

A ① I'd like to, but I can't.
  ② I want to go to a movie today.
  ③ There is a good movie in the theater.
  ④ Let's play outside next time.

C ① I'd love to, but I can't.
  ② I have a cold and I feel sleepy.
  ③ I want to rest.
  ④ So I can't go outside.

A

You want to go to a movie today. There is a good movie in the theater. You want to see that movie today. But your friend wants to play outside with you. What would you like to say to him?

당신은 오늘 영화를 보러 가고 싶습니다. 영화관에서는 재미있는 영화가 상영 중입니다. 당신은 오늘 그 영화를 보고 싶습니다. 그런데 당신의 친구가 당신과 밖에서 놀고 싶어합니다. 당신은 그에게 뭐라고 말하겠습니까?

① I'd like to, but I can't.
나도 그러고 싶지만 안될 것 같아.

② I want to go to a movie today.
난 오늘 영화를 보러 가고 싶어.

③ There is a good movie in the theater.
영화관에 좋은 영화 한 편이 상영 중이야.

④ Let's play outside next time.
다음 번에 나가서 놀자.

C

You have a cold and you feel sleepy. You want to rest. But your friend calls you. She wants to have lunch outside with you. What would you like to say to your friend?

당신은 감기에 걸렸고, 또 졸리기도 합니다. 당신은 쉬고 싶습니다. 그런데 당신의 친구가 당신에게 전화를 했습니다. 그녀는 당신과 밖에서 점심을 먹고 싶어합니다. 당신은 친구에게 뭐라고 말하겠습니까?

① I'd love to, but I can't.
나도 정말 그러고 싶지만 안돼.

② I have a cold and I feel sleepy.
나는 감기에 걸렸고 졸려.

③ I want to rest.
나 쉬고 싶어.

④ So I can't go outside.
그래서 나는 밖에 나갈 수 없어.

단원 평가   pp.112-113

A

You and your friends are going to play baseball this afternoon. But your mother wants to go shopping with you. You can't go shopping with your mother because of the baseball game. What would you say to your mother?

당신과 당신의 친구들은 오늘 오후에 야구를 하려고 합니다. 그런데 당신의 어머니가 당신과 쇼핑을 가고 싶어합니다. 야구 경기 때문에 당신은 어머니와 쇼핑을 갈 수 없습니다. 당신은 어머니께 뭐라고 말하겠습니까?

I'm sorry, mom. I'd love to go shopping with you, but I promised to play baseball with my friends this afternoon. Shall we go shopping tomorrow?

죄송해요, 엄마. 엄마랑 같이 쇼핑 가고 싶지만, 오늘 오후에 친구들이랑 야구를 하기로 약속했어요. 내일 같이 갈까요?

be going to ~을 하려고 한다 / play baseball 야구를 하다 /
this afternoon 오늘 오후 / go shopping 쇼핑 가다 /
can't 할 수 없다 / because of ~ 때문에 /
baseball game 야구 게임 /
What would you say to ~? ~에게 뭐라고 말하겠습니까?

친구와 먼저 한 약속이 있기 때문에 엄마의 요청을 거절하는 메시지를 작성해야 합니다. 우선 미안하다는 표현으로 시작하고, 하고 싶지만 할 수 없는 이유를 말하고, '내일 가는 게 어떤지'로 마무리를 지어 말해보세요.

B

You are in the library. You are reading a book. It is interesting. Your friend asks you to go out to eat something. But you want to finish this book. What would you like to say to your friend?

당신은 도서관에 있습니다. 당신은 책을 읽는 중입니다. 그 책은 재미있습니다. 당신의 친구가 당신에게 뭘 좀 먹으러 나가자고 말합니다. 하지만 당신은 이 책을 끝내고 싶습니다. 당신은 친구에게 뭐라고 말하겠습니까?

I'm sorry, but I can't go out now. I am reading this book and I want to finish it. I can go out to eat after I finish this book.

미안하지만 지금 나갈 수가 없어. 지금 책을 읽는 중인데, 이 책을 다 끝내고 싶어. 이 책 다 읽고 나면 먹으러 나갈 수 있어.

library 도서관 / interesting 흥미로운 / ask 요청하다 /
go out 밖에 나가다 / to eat something 뭔가를 먹으러 /
finish 끝내다 / What would you like to say to ~? ~에게 뭐라 말하고 싶습니까?

지금 읽는 책을 끝까지 다 읽고 싶기 때문에 친구의 요청을 거절하는 메시지를 작성해야 합니다. 우선 미안하다는 표현으로 시작하고, 하고 싶지만 할 수 없는 이유를 자세히 말해 보세요.

Unit 12 부탁하기

표현 연습 pp.114-115

A
1. Would you lift this box for me? /
   Could you lift this box for me?
2. Would you open the door for me? /
   Could you open the door for me?
3. May I borrow your pencil? /
   Could I borrow your pencil?
4. May I use your eraser? /
   Could I use your eraser?

C
1. Would you / Could you
2. Would you / Could you
3. May I / Could I
4. May I / Could I

A

1. Would you lift this box for me? This box is too heavy for me.

   저를 위해 이 상자 좀 들어주시겠어요? 이 상자가 저에게는 너무 무거워요.

   Could you lift this box for me? This box is too heavy for me.

   저를 위해 이 상자 좀 들어주시겠어요? 이 상자가 저에게는 너무 무거워요.

2. <u>Would you open the door for me?</u> I have too many books in my hands.
저를 위해 문 좀 열어 주시겠어요? 제가 손에 책이 너무 많아서요.

<u>Could you open the door for me?</u> I have too many books in my hands.
저를 위해 문 좀 열어 주시겠어요? 제가 손에 책이 너무 많아서요.

3. <u>May I borrow your pencil?</u> I can't find my pencil.
제가 당신의 연필을 좀 빌려도 될까요? 제 연필을 찾을 수가 없네요.

<u>Could I borrow your pencil?</u> I can't find my pencil.
제가 당신의 연필을 좀 빌려도 될까요? 제 연필을 찾을 수가 없네요.

4. <u>May I use your eraser?</u> I don't have one.
제가 당신의 지우개를 좀 빌려도 될까요? 제게 지우개가 없어서요.

<u>Could I use your eraser?</u> I don't have one.
제가 당신의 지우개를 좀 빌려도 될까요? 제게 지우개가 없어서요.

C

1. A: <u>Would you</u> say that one more time?
   <u>Could you</u> say that one more time?
   B: No problem.

   A: 그것을 한번 더 말씀해 주시겠어요?
   B: 그럼요.

2. A: <u>Would you</u> give me some water?
   <u>Could you</u> give me some water?
   B: Certainly.

   A: 제게 물을 좀 주시겠어요?
   B: 그럼요.

3. A: <u>May I</u> sit here?
   <u>Could I</u> sit here?
   B: Yes, of course.

   A: 제가 여기 앉아도 될까요?
   B: 네, 물론이죠.

4. A: <u>May I</u> join your soccer game?
   <u>Could I</u> join your soccer game?
   B: Sure.

   A: 내가 너의 축구팀에 들어가도 될까?
   B: 물론이지.

기본 말하기　　　　　p.116

A ① how are you　　② looking for
　　③ can't find it　　④ Would you help me

A

① Hi, <u>how are you</u>?
안녕하세요?

② I am <u>looking for</u> the book, "The History of Korea."
저는 "한국의 역사"라는 책을 찾고 있어요.

③ But I <u>can't find it</u> in this section.
그런데 이 구역에서 그 책을 찾을 수가 없네요.

④ <u>Would you help me</u> find the book?
제가 책을 찾는 것을 도와주시겠어요?

심화 말하기　　　　　p.117

A ① Would you help me solve this question?
　　② This question is too difficult.
　　③ So I can't solve it.
　　④ Would you help me with my homework?

A

You are doing your math homework. But it is too difficult. You need someone's help. You can ask your mother to help you. What would you like to say to your mother?

당신은 수학 숙제 중입니다. 하지만 매우 어렵습니다. 당신은 누군가의 도움이 필요합니다. 당신은 어머니께 도와 달라고 부탁할 수 있습니다. 당신은 어머니께 뭐라고 말하겠습니까?

① Would you help me solve this question?
이 문제 푸는 것을 도와주실래요?

② This question is too difficult.
이 문제는 너무 어려워요.

③ So I can't solve it.
그래서 풀 수가 없어요.

④ Would you help me with my homework?
제 숙제를 도와주시겠어요?

실전 유형 대비하기 pp.118-119

A ① I'm sorry mom, but I am hungry.
　② Would you make me some food?
　③ I want to eat something.
　④ Thank you very much.

C ① Would you buy me ice cream
　② I have an English word test tomorrow
　③ So I am busy now.
　④ Thank you so much!

A

You are studying. You are hungry. You want to eat something, but your mother is watching TV. What would you like to say to your mother?

당신은 공부하는 중입니다. 당신은 배가 고픕니다. 당신은 뭔가를 먹고 싶지만, 어머니께서는 TV를 보고 계십니다. 당신은 어머니께 뭐라고 말하겠습니까?

① I'm sorry mom, but I am hungry.
엄마 죄송한데, 저 지금 배가 고파요.

② Would you make me some food?
음식 좀 만들어주시겠어요?

③ I want to eat something.
뭐가 좀 먹고 싶어요.

④ Thank you very much.
감사해요.

C

You are studying. You have an English word test tomorrow. You want to eat ice cream, but you can't go out because you are busy. Your brother will go to a supermarket to buy something. What would you like to say to your brother?

당신은 공부하는 중입니다. 당신은 내일 영어 단어 시험이 있습니다. 당신은 아이스크림을 먹고 싶지만, 바빠서 나갈 수가 없습니다. 당신의 남동생이 뭔가를 사러 슈퍼마켓에 갈 것입니다. 당신은 남동생에게 뭐라고 말하겠습니까?

① Would you buy me ice cream at the supermarket?
슈퍼마켓에서 아이스크림 좀 사다 줄 수 있어?

② I am studying because I have an English word test tomorrow.
내일 영어 단어 시험이 있어서 난 지금 공부를 하고 있어.

③ So I am busy now.
그래서 지금 바빠.

④ Thank you so much!
고마워!

단원 평가 pp.120-121

A

You have a computer. It is old. Sometimes it doesn't work well. You want to buy a new one. You can ask your mother to buy a new computer. What would you like to say to your mother?

당신에게는 컴퓨터가 한 대 있습니다. 그것은 낡았습니다. 그 컴퓨터는 가끔씩 작동을 잘 하지 않습니다. 당신은 새 컴퓨터를 사고 싶습니다. 당신은 어머니께 새 컴퓨터를 사달라고 부탁할 수 있습니다. 당신은 어머니께 뭐라고 말하겠습니까?

Mom, I'd like to change this computer to a new one. This computer is too old. I need a new computer because it doesn't work well. I want to use a new computer. Would you buy me a new computer?

엄마, 저 이 컴퓨터 새 걸로 바꾸고 싶어요. 이 컴퓨터는 너무 오래됐어요. 컴퓨터가 작동이 잘 안 돼서 새 컴퓨터가 필요해요. 새 컴퓨터를 쓰고 싶어요. 제게 새 컴퓨터를 사주시겠어요?

old 낡은 / sometimes 가끔 / work well 잘 작동하다 / buy 사주다 / What would you like to say to ~? ~에게 뭐라 말하고 싶습니까? / one (어떤) 것 / I'd like to ~. 나는 ~하고 싶어요. / change ~ to ~을 ~로 바꾸다 / too 너무 / new 새로운 / because 왜냐면 / use 사용하다 / Would you buy me ~? 저에게 ~을 사주시겠어요?

낡은 컴퓨터가 잘 작동하지 않아 엄마에게 새것을 사줄 수 있는지 부탁하는 메시지를 작성해야 합니다. 우선 무엇을 원하는지와 그 이유를 자세히 말하고 마지막에 정중히 부탁하는 표현을 말해보세요.

B

It's raining. You don't have an umbrella with you. You can't go home because of heavy rain. Nobody has an umbrella around you. You want to ask your mother to bring an umbrella. What would you like to say to your mother?

비가 오고 있습니다. 당신에게는 지금 우산이 없습니다. 폭우 때문에 당신은 집에 갈 수 없습니다. 주변에 아무도 우산을 가진 사람이 없습니다. 당신은 어머니께 우산을 가져다 달라고 부탁하고 싶습니다. 당신은 어머니께 뭐라고 말하겠습니까?

Mom, it is raining, but I don't have an umbrella. I can't go back home now. Would you bring me an umbrella? I am in front of the library building. Thank you.

엄마, 지금 비가 오는데, 제게 우산이 없어요. 지금 집으로 갈 수가 없어요. 우산 좀 갖다 주시겠어요? 지금 도서관 건물 앞에 있어요. 고맙습니다.

raining 비가 오고 있는 / umbrella 우산 / can't go home 집에 갈 수가 없다 / because of ~때문에 / heavy rain 거센 비 / nobody 아무도 / around you 당신 주위에 / ask 부탁하다 / bring 가져오다 / What would you like to say to ~? ~에게 뭐라 말하고 싶습니까? / Would you ~? 당신이 ~해주시겠어요? / in front of ~앞에 / library building 도서관 건물

거센 비가 오는데 우산이 없어 집에 갈 수 없는 상황에서 엄마에게 우산을 가지고 데리러 와주시길 부탁하는 메시지를 작성해야 합니다. 우선 현재 나의 상황을 자세히 알리고, 엄마에게 부탁의 내용을 말한 뒤 감사의 표현을 말해보세요.

실전 유형 평가   pp.124-127

1. 그림 보고 질문에 답하기

Q a: What is the boy doing?
소년은 무엇을 하고 있나요?

He is studying.
그는 공부를 하고 있습니다.

He is studying in the library.
그는 도서관에서 공부를 하고 있습니다.

what 무엇 / doing 하고 있는 / studying 공부하고 있는 / in the library 도서관에서

그림 속 소년이 무엇을 하고 있는지를 묘사해야 하는 문제이므로 우선 그림 속 소년이 무엇을 보고 있고, 무엇을 하고 있는지를 파악해야 합니다. 소년이 눈으로 보고 있는 것은 책들이고, 손은 필기를 하는 것을 보아 소년은 공부를 하고 있으며 장소

는 도서관이므로 이를 현재 진행 시제인 'He / is studying / in the library.' 라고 말하세요.

Q b: Is the girl happy?
　　소녀는 행복한가요?

No, she isn't.
아니요.

No, she isn't happy.
아니요, 그녀는 행복하지 않습니다.

No, she isn't. She is crying.
아니요, 그녀는 울고 있습니다.

happy 기분 좋은 / crying 울고 있는

그림의 내용은 한 소녀가 엄마에게 혼나고 울고 있는 모습이므로 '소녀는 기분이 좋은가요?' 라는 be동사 Yes / No 의문문에 일단 '아니요, 그렇지 않습니다.' 즉, 'No, she isn't.' 라고 말합니다. 그리고 나서 '그녀는 울고 있어요.' 라는 내용을 현재 진행 시제인 'She / is crying.' 이라고 말하세요.

Q c: Where are they?
　　그들은 어디에 있나요?

They are in the restaurant.
그들은 식당에 있습니다.

where 어디 / in the restaurant 식당 안에

그들이 어디에 있는지를 묻고 있으므로 그림 속 주인공들이 있는 장소를 살펴 봅니다. 하얀 식탁보가 차려진 잘 꾸며진 공간에서 식사를 하는 것으로 보아 그들은 식당 안에 있습니다. 그러므로 'They are / in the restaurant.' 이라고 말하세요.

2. 연계 질문에 답하기

Q a: What time shall we meet?
　　우리 언제 만날까요?

Let's meet at 1 o'clock.
1시에 만납시다.

How about 1 o'clock?
1시는 어때요?

what time 몇 시 / Shall we ~? ~할까요? / meet 만나다 /
Let's ~. ~하자. / o'clock (몇) 시 /
How about ~? ~는 어때요?

'우리 몇 시에 만날까?' 라는 질문이므로 'Let's meet / at 1 o'clock.' 또는 'How about / 1 o'clock?' 처럼 '몇 시' 에 대한 내용을 넣어서 완전한 문장으로 답하세요.

Q b: What would you like for lunch?
　　점심으로 뭘 먹고 싶은가요?

I want to eat pizza.
피자를 먹고 싶어요.

I'd like to have kimchi jjigae.
김치찌개를 먹고 싶어요.

what 무엇 / would you like~? ~을 좋아하니? /
for lunch 점심식사로 / I'd like to ~. 나는 ~을 하고 싶다. /
have 먹다

무엇을 먹고 싶냐는 질문이므로 'I / want to eat / pizza.' 또는 'I'd like to have / kimchi jjigae.' 처럼 '무엇' 에 대한 내용을 넣어서 완전한 문장으로 답하세요.

Q c: Why do you like it?
　　왜 그 음식을 좋아하나요?

It is delicious.
맛이 있어서요.

It is my favorite food.
그것은 내가 무척 좋아하는 음식이에요.

why 왜 / delicious 맛있는 / favorite 가장 좋아하는 /
food 음식

해설

왜 그 음식을 좋아하냐는 질문이므로 'It is delicious.' 또는
'It is my favorite food.' 처럼 '왜' 에 대한 이유를 넣어서 완
전한 문장으로 답하세요.

Q d: Where shall we go?
　　어디로 갈까요?

모범 답안

Let's go to Kelly's, an Italian restaurant.
켈리스라는 이탈리아 레스토랑으로 가요.

How about the Korean restaurant?
한국 식당 어때요?

필수 어휘

where 어디 / Shall we ~? ~할까요? /
Let's go to ~. ~로 갑시다. /
Italian restaurant 이탈리아 요리 식당 /
How about ~? ~는 어때요? /
Korean restaurant 한국 요리 식당

해설

'어디로 갈까요?' 라는 질문이므로 'Let's go / to Kelly's, /
an Italian restaurant.' 또는 'How about / the Korean
restaurant?' 처럼 '어디' 에 대한 내용을 넣어서 완전한 문장
으로 답하세요.

3. 그림 묘사하기

① A boy is in a hospital.
　한 소년이 병원에 와있다.

② A doctor checks the boy.
　의사가 소년을 진료한다.

③ The doctor says, "It will be all right."
　의사가 "괜찮아질 거야"라고 말한다.

④ The nurse comes into the room.
　간호사가 진료실에 들어온다.

⑤ Then, the nurse gives the boy a shot.
　그리고 나서, 간호사가 소년에게 주사를 놓는다.

⑥ Finally, the boy comes out of the hospital.
　마침내, 소년은 병원에서 나온다.

전체 그림 묘사 내용

A boy is in a hospital. A doctor checks the boy. The
doctor says, "It will be all right." The nurse comes
into the room. Then, the nurse gives the boy a shot.
Finally, the boy comes out of the hospital.

필수 어휘

hospital 병원 / check 진찰하다 /
It will be all right. 괜찮아질 거예요. / nurse 간호사 /
comes into ~안으로 들어오다 / room 방 / then 그리고 나서
/ give a shot 주사를 놓다 / finally 마침내 /
come out of ~로부터 나오다

해설

6개의 그림을 보고 이야기를 구성하기 위해서는 모든 그림을
본 뒤 하나의 이어지는 이야기를 만들어야 합니다. 첫 번째 그
림의 중요 표현은 'in a hospital', 두 번째 그림의 중요 표현
은 'A doctor checks', 세 번째 그림의 중요 표현은 "It
will be all right.", 네 번째 그림의 중요 표현은 'The nurse
comes', 다섯 번째 그림의 중요 표현은 'the nurse gives
the boy a shot.', 여섯 번째 그림의 중요 표현은 'come
out of the hospital' 입니다. 이 때 단순 현재 시제로 말하도
록 하며, 주어가 3인칭 단수일 때 동사가 3인칭 변화하는 것을
잊지 말고 말하세요.

4. 문제 해결하기

One of your friends asks you to go to the movies
tonight. But you and your mom will go to a concert.
So you can't go see a movie with your friend. What
would you say to your friend?

당신의 친구 한 명이 오늘 밤에 영화를 보러 가자고 물어봅니
다. 하지만 당신과 당신의 엄마는 음악회에 갈 것입니다. 그래
서 당신은 친구와 영화를 보러 갈 수가 없습니다. 당신은 친구
에게 뭐라고 말하겠습니까?

I'm sorry, but I can't. I need to go to a concert with my mom tonight. So I can't go to the movies. Let's go to a movie next time!

미안하지만 안될 것 같아. 나는 오늘밤 엄마와 음악회에 가야 해. 그래서 영화 보러 못 가. 다음에 영화 보러 가자.

필수 어휘

one of your friends 당신의 친구들 중 한 명 / ask 묻다 /
go to the movies 영화관에 가다 / tonight 오늘밤 /
concert 음악회 / so 그래서 / can't 할 수 없다 /
see a movie 영화를 보다 /
What would you say to ~? ~에게 뭐라고 말하겠습니까?

해설

친구가 오늘밤 영화를 보러 가자고 하는데 이미 엄마와 음악회에 가기로 해서 친구와 영화를 볼 수 없는 상황이라 친구의 요청을 거절하는 메시지를 작성해야 합니다. 우선 미안함을 표시하고 왜 갈 수 없는지 상황을 잘 말하도록 합니다. 그런 뒤 '하지만 다음 번에 영화관에 가자'고 마무리를 지어 말하세요.

MEMO

MEMO

MEMO